FESTIVAL
FEVER

First published 2017 by The O'Brien Press Ltd,
12 Terenure Road East, Rathgar,
Dublin 6, D06 HD27, Ireland.
Tel: +353 1 4923333; Fax: +353 1 4922777
E-mail: books@obrien.ie
Website: www.obrien.ie
The O'Brien Press is a member of Publishing Ireland.

ISBN: 978-1-84717-956-2

Text © Anne Holland 2017
Editing, typesetting, layout, design © The O'Brien Press Ltd

8 7 6 5 4 3 2 1
21 20 19 18 17

Printed and bound by Gutenberg Press, Malta.
The paper in this book is produced using pulp from managed forests.

Front cover photo: Sizing John, ridden by Robbie Power, on their way to victory in the 2017
Cheltenham Gold Cup (Racehorse Photos).
Back cover photos:
Top left: Arkle enjoying his daily Guinness; top middle: Dawn Run ridden by Charmian Hill;
top right: Jockey Davy Russell shows his affection for Presenting Percy; bottom left: Hardy
Eustace in mid-flight, piloted by Conor O'Dwyer; bottom right: Newmill and Andrew
McNamara on their way to Queen Mother Champion Chase victory (all courtesy of Healy
Racing).

Picture credits
Photo section 1:
Healy Racing: p.1, all; p.2, top and bottom; p,3, both; p.4, both; p.5, all; p.6, all; p.7, both; p.8, all.
Racehorse Photos: p.2, middle; p.8, top.
Photo section 2:
Healy Racing: p.1, both; p.3, bottom left and right; p.4, all; p.5, bottom; p.6, bottom left and
right; p.7, bottom; p.8, top left and bottom.
Racehorse Photos: p.2, all; p.3, top; p.5, top; p.7, top; p.8, top right.

Published in

DUBLIN
UNESCO
City of Literature

FESTIVAL FEVER

THE IRISH
AT CHELTENHAM

ANNE HOLLAND

THE O'BRIEN PRESS
DUBLIN

ACKNOWLEDGEMENTS

My sincere thanks to all of the following, for their openness, kindness and spirit of co-operation in helping me to make this book a reality:

Joan Barry; Elizabeth Anne – Dotty – Benson; Henry de Bromhead; Andrew Brookings; Father Jimmy Browne; Sofia Brudenell, Cheltenham Racecourse Publicity; Rory Campbell; Simon Claisse, Regional Head of Racing, South West, and Clerk of the Course; the Colesbourne Inn; Louise Cooper-Joyce; for Dean Close School, Cheltenham: David Evans, Senior Master, Alex Hume, Old Decanian Liaison Officer, Grace Pritchard-Woods, Archivist, Charles Whitney, School Historian; Mark Costello, *The Irish Field;* Geraldine Counihan; Sofie Dale, Cheltenham PRO; Magda Dunlop; Nick Dunlop; Gordon Elliott; Evelyn, Jo and Catriona, Willie Mullins' office; Noel Fehily; Mick Foster; Malcolm Fraser, patience personified, who cooked while I wrote; Edward Gillespie, former CEO of Cheltenham Racecourse; Jessica Harrington; Eddie Harty; Ger Hennelly; Robbie Hennessy; Val Joyce, author of the song *Dawn Run;* Hughie Kane; Sheila Kelly; Jack Kennedy; Ollie Kennedy, composer for the song *Dawn Run;* Nicole Kent; Andrew Lynch; Matt McElhone; Peter McNeile, former marketing manager, Cheltenham Racecourse; Liam Metcalf, Blackrock Hospice; Paul Metcalfe; Mouse Morris; Maureen Mullins; Willie Mullins; Colm Murphy; Keith Neville; Cliff Noone, Press Officer, Irish Turf Club; Seamus O'Connor; Jacqueline O'Neill; Jonjo O'Neill; Nick Peacock; Charles Powell; Nial Redmond; Geoff Davis, of the Sallynoggin Inn, Dun Laoghaire; Gavin Sheehan; Jim Sheridan; Tom Taaffe; Gary Thornton; Zoe Winston and Michael Worcester.

CONTENTS

AUTHOR'S NOTE

The Irish are synonymous with Cheltenham but, perhaps surprisingly, this was not always so; it took a positive stance from the management to encourage more Irish horses to come over, and with them an increased number of Irish visitors.

The array of tales here of Irish horses at Cheltenham, the stables associated with them and the many and diverse Irish visitors, can only illustrate an across-the-board sample, a tempting morsel, describing feats on the racecourse and some of the experiences off it. It has been a privilege to be shown round yards both big and small, and to meet people both famous and not so – all with one common denominator: special memories of the Cheltenham Festival. I have concentrated on the twenty-first century, with an overview of the event before then – if everyone and every horse worthy of it were to be mentioned, this book would be little more than a long list.

I am hugely indebted to the many people who have given of their time and willingly told their stories for inclusion here.

A.H.

July 2017

CHAPTER 1

ENTICING THE

IRISH

'Will the last person out of Ireland please turn off the lights' – sign spotted in Dublin Airport, mid-March.

'In March, each year the land level in Ireland rises a few feet, because everyone's left for Cheltenham.' Matt McElhone, Wiltshire garage proprietor whose family hails from County Leitrim.

At times, it certainly does seem as if the whole population has crossed the water to the Cheltenham Festival. Dozens of extra flights are slotted into a number of middle-England airports to accommodate demand, including some thirty by Ryanair to Birmingham.

Festival fervour is in evidence well before Christmas, and by early March has reached fever pitch. Irish sports headlines are dominated by the chances of the Irish horses, and almost the whole of Ireland, it seems, attends a Cheltenham preview night – this is not just in rural Ireland, but also at venues around Dublin, Cork and all the cities. It really is the whole of Ireland that takes Cheltenham to its heart.

And no wonder. This is where the very best of horseflesh from either side of the Irish Sea (and occasionally from France) pit their wits against each other to determine the best three-mile chaser for the top accolade, the Cheltenham Gold Cup. There is the exciting speed of the Queen Mother Champion Chase and of the Champion Hurdles, both over two miles, and the stamina crown on offer for the winner of the Stayers' Hurdle.

Many of the visitors will be evaluating the chances of 'their' horses in the various handicaps, filling the bars on the course and the hotels and inns of the area at night, poring over the form and making their betting choices. And when the flag drops for the opening Supreme Novices' Hurdle, the roar of 66,000 people can surely be heard a mile away. None of them could have imagined just how successful Ireland would be in 2017.

Cheltenham Racecourse sits in Prestbury Park, on the outskirts of the gracious spa town, and is guarded over by mighty Cleeve Hill on the edge of the Cotswolds, making the racecourse bowl below resemble an amphitheatre. For the last twelve months, trainers, jockeys and owners have dreamt the dream of having a runner – or better, a winner – at the Festival; Joe Public will have spent six months following horses that might be Cheltenham-bound, and he, too, will feel a tingle down his spine as he enters the milling throng that abounds inside the racecourse.

The twenty-first century has seen more Irish winners than ever before, but the Irish–English rivalry is nearly as old as the Festival itself. Even before Vincent O'Brien barnstormed the Festival in the late 1940s and early 1950s, there had been a scattering of Irish-trained winners.

To qualify as an Irish win, a horse has to be trained in Ireland; if this were not the case, Ireland throughout the ages would often have topped the table, as so many Irish-bred horses are sold to England and trained there, their victories then going down as English. An example would be an Irish-bred horse, owned by JP McManus, ridden by Barry Geraghty and trained by Jonjo O'Neill, all as Irish as they come – but Jonjo trains in England – in fact in the Cotswolds, just a stone's throw from Prestbury Park – and so it goes down as an English winner.

Although it may seem that all the racing fans of Ireland attend the annual National Hunt Festival at Cheltenham, the increase in the last number of decades did not come about entirely by chance or through simple enthusiasm. Sure, there was a healthy Irish–English rivalry, but for a long time it was mainly those connected with runners who came over. Run-of-the-mill racegoers had plenty of Irish tracks to attend themselves.

In 1989, there was no Irish-trained winner at Cheltenham, and only one in each of the previous two years (Galmoy, trained by John Mulhern and ridden by Tommy Carmody, in the Stayers' Hurdle both times). It was then that the Cheltenham executive became concerned, and set about enticing more Irish runners over. One problem identified was the comparative softness of Irish steeplechase fences compared to the much firmer ones at Cheltenham; Irish horses weren't used to them, and found them harder to negotiate.

One practical step was for Cheltenham to take a stand at major Irish meetings, complete with a section of steeplechase fence, with Cheltenham's then chief executive Edward Gillespie undertaking a charm offensive. Irish racecourses began to copy the fences, and, in some measure at least, this led to the turnaround in Irish fortunes at the Festival.

Another problem was the discrepancy in some rules between British and Irish racing, such as in the use of the whip. A rule had been introduced in England limiting the number of strikes a jockey could give with his whip, especially after the last fence. As Irish jockeys were not used to this, Cheltenham racecourse moved the last fence a little nearer the finishing line, leaving a shorter run-in and therefore less opportunity for jockeys to give too many strikes with the whip. It must be added that the whip itself has today been altered drastically, so that it is little more than a soft pad; a horse may be encouraged but not hurt by it.

This dearth of Irish winners also coincided with the Iran–Iraq war, and that conflict was stealing the headlines. This made it difficult for Peter McNeile, the then marketing manager of Cheltenham, to gain photo opportunities, so he organised a syndicated series about the Festival to newspapers large and small all over Ireland. The result was that tiny, maybe spurious, titles began applying for and being granted Press accreditation to the Festival, and their reports and photographs in turn stimulated more Irish to come to subsequent Festivals.

Another ruse was to take parties of accredited British newspaper racing journalists over to Ireland. This was in the days when there were dedicated racing desks on all the national newspapers.

One visit was to Aidan O'Brien's stable when he was training Istabraq, three times winner of the Champion Hurdle, and before Aidan became the big Flat player that he is today.

Such trips enabled both trainers and journalists to get to know and trust each other in quality time, strengthening media relations, which could be valuable should something contentious occur at the Festival. The Irish press were also invited to these events. One such occasion saw the launch of the Anglo-Irish Bank as sponsors of the Supreme Novices' Hurdle at the Dunraven Arms, a sporting hotel in Adare, County Limerick. This is only a mile or two from trainer Michael Hourigan, who gained his first Cheltenham winner with Doran's Pride in the 1995 Stayers' Hurdle. One memory of the occasion for Peter McNeile was of one of Michael's sons 'taking loads of money off the visiting journalists with a three-glass trick'.

On another occasion, the party was being entertained to lunch by Michael Smurfit at his world-renowned K Club in Straffan, County Kildare. This is a magnificent nineteenth-century mansion, set in 550 acres, home to two championship golf courses and bounded on one side by the River Liffey. Michael Smurfit converted it to a five-star hotel in 1991, and in 2006 achieved his dream of hosting the Ryder Cup there. It was about halfway through the meal with the racing press that Peter McNeile noticed their host was being plied with a separate, superior bottle of wine.

'Michael Smurfit was a game-changer for sponsorship,' Peter McNeile recalls, 'and led to many Irish sponsorships, helped by the Celtic Tiger.'

Former Cheltenham chief executive Edward Gillespie agrees, and recalls his own dealings when securing the Smurfit sponsorship for the Champion Hurdle.

He was accompanying the then Cheltenham chairman Lord Vestey, and Michael Smurfit also had the chief executive of his packaging company with him. Lunch was again in the K Club.

In typically Irish fashion, just about every subject under the sun was discussed, except for the main one. Golf, politics, golf again, medical matters, more golf … Every time Edward tried to steer conversation round to the Champion Hurdle, it went off at another tangent – usually golf.

After two-and-a-half hours – Michael Smurfit with his own wine – they reached coffee, and suddenly Michael Smurfit came out with, 'What I'd like to do is this: three years of this … and two years of that …'

'Great,' said Sam Vestey, and the two men shook hands; that was that, and Michael Smurfit left. When he had gone, Michael Smurfit's chief asked Edward Gillespie, 'What have we just agreed?' Edward filled him in, and the sponsorship became one of Cheltenham's most successful.

It had a knock-on effect, too. One year, Michael Smurfit and George Ward, whose Grunwick Group sponsored the Bonus Print Stayers' Hurdle, were dining in the Royal Box and chatting about their respective businesses. The upshot was that Smurfit secured the contract for the packaging of Grunwick products.

The Festival was attended one year by Mary McAleese when she was President of Ireland, along with half of the Irish Rugby team. They came on the Thursday, prior to playing England at Twickenham on the Saturday.

British-based Irish companies bring not only lots of entertainment to the Festival, but also considerable sponsorship. They love Cheltenham's unique flavour and recognise that uniqueness in promotions.

Most such sponsorship deals have been made in Dublin, with firms like Guinness, the *Irish Times*, *Independent* and *Star*. Peter McNeile remembers the sales rep of the 'Indo', Eugene Fitzsimmons, well, 'a charming guy who loved his racing, like so many of them'.

Today, Ryanair supports the top two-mile five-furlong steeplechase, and its boss, Michael O'Leary, along with his brother Eddie, have become huge racehorse owners in Ireland under their Gigginstown House Stud banner. In days gone by, the Champion Hurdle was sponsored by the now-defunct Waterford Crystal, and then by Smurfit/Kappa Smurfit.

The *Irish Independent* was a long-standing sponsor of the Arkle Chase, and Guinness has been a sponsor of the Guinness Enclosure for twenty-five years; this includes a temporary seated grandstand opposite the final fence, and a whole village of assorted trade stands. Some 265,000 pints of Guinness are drunk during each Festival. The *Irish Independent* now sponsors the Leading Owner award.

Another successful scheme to entice more Irish participation from the 1980s was a free race-card given with the *Independent* in the UK – a logistical challenge to get cards for the day's Festival inside some 20,000 papers in the early hours. This was aimed at people watching from home, including many ex-pat Irish. It resulted in scores of them coming to the Festival in person the following year, and this in turn fuelled the Festival's popularity. The Festival made a big impact on circulation, so the 'freebie' brought a tangible return to both parties, a win–win situation.

Peter McNeile adds, 'All the Irish winners are a great thing for the Festival, including with the English. The Irish love competition, plus the spirit of adventure in coming over here. It is remarkable that such a small country can deliver such a large impact, not just commercially but also emotionally. They embraced the Festival and took it to their hearts. The Irish are also very pleasant to deal with and quite straightforward – but great characters, too.'

Another ploy was to offer generous travel grants to the connections of possible Irish runners. This worked like clockwork, bringing the number of Irish runners up to a steady seventy to eighty horses per year, of which approximately ten percent won.

Since the early 2000s, these figures have increased year on year – 2006 was the first time that Irish winners reached double figures, and in 2008, the Irish brought 124 horses, the first time the number topped 100, and they won eight races. With the exception of 2011, when there were ninety-seven Irish horses, the number of Irish runners has consistently been more than 100, the most being in 2015, when 155 Irish runners brought them thirteen wins. In 2017, the percentage of Irish wins in the twenty-eight races was a fraction under seventy percent, a phenomenal feat for a tiny nation. These wins came not only via the bandwagons of Willie Mullins' mighty stable and, increasingly, that of Gordon Elliott, but also included a steady stream of winners from stables that house a bare handful of horses.

Edward Gillespie, former Cheltenham CEO, says, 'The Irish boys have always been great. For instance, when low sun was threatening to omit a fence, they wanted to continue.'

'The Irish are an essential part of the DNA at Cheltenham, and there is mutual respect.' Edward Gillespie

A TRUCKFUL OF TROPHIES

On the Saturday and Monday before the start of the Festival, the office is awash with Irish owners and trainers, picking up tickets, asking questions and so on.

Some Irish bring their own water for their horses, and others ask for spring water, which Cheltenham can provide via one of its vets, who has a spring on his land.

One of the most unusual requests came one year on the Saturday after racing, when a pick-up van had to be used to transport all Willie Mullins' trophies up to one of his brother George's horse transport lorries, because Willie's car boot was too small to take them all.

A TALL TALE

In 1995, essential drainage work was to be carried out in Prestbury village after the Festival, causing the usual April and May Cheltenham race meetings to be cancelled. As some compensation, a fourth Festival day was trialled (it was to be another decade before a fourth day was added permanently), and this happened to land on St Patrick's Day, 17 March. With Guinness already well involved at the Festival, the executive decided to give the day an Irish theme by commemorating the first ever steeplechase on either side of the water, staged across country from Buttevant to Doneraile, County Cork, in 1752. So, among the races scheduled for that day was the Buttevant Hunters Chase and the Doneraile Handicap Hurdle.

Such planning is flagged well in advance. One day in the previous autumn, Peter McNeile took a call in his office from someone with a distinctly Irish brogue.

'I see you have a Buttevant hunters steeplechase,' he said. 'Well, I'm the Mayor of Buttevant. Have you got anyone to present the trophy?'

This was probably low on Peter McNeile's priority list, and so the answer was no.

'Well, I'd like to present it on behalf of the town.'

'Nice idea,' agreed Peter, 'we'll talk nearer the time, when I'll know if we have a sponsor.'

The Irishman rang again in February. There was no sponsor for the race, and so it was agreed that he could present the trophy.

About a week before the Festival another Irishman rang, this time from Doneraile. Was he the Mayor of that town about to ask to do similar honours for the Doneraile Hurdle? Not a bit of it.

'I have to tell you,' he told Peter McNeile, 'that there is no Mayor of Buttevant.'

Nevertheless, Peter decided it would be harmless, and he let the presentation continue as planned, the ticket having doubtless already been sent out. On the day, an unprepossessing chubby chap turned up in a raincoat, but there was a twinkle in his eye as he presented the trophy.

'It would make good pictures for his grandchildren,' Peter smiled, rather admiring the Irishman's bold brassiness.

DISEASE BRINGS DELICATE AND DIFFICULT DAYS

In the spring of 2001, the United Kingdom was rocked by an outbreak of virulent foot and mouth disease, not seen in the country since 1967. It caused devastation in the countryside, especially through the losses of flocks and herds that had taken generations to breed into prime stock. Horse owners could be thankful that their pride and joys could not catch it, but they can be carriers, and firm restrictions were imposed.

Cheltenham was in turmoil. Will the Festival be held? Or won't it? Can it? Can't it? What if the Irish aren't there? The Irish authorities imposed a blanket ban on their horses travelling to anywhere in the UK. Cheltenham at this time was not in a restricted area – in theory, the Festival could go ahead. But the Festival without the Irish was unthinkable.

Irish trainers, understandably, became agitated – Irish owners thought the Festival was going ahead without them. The Cheltenham executive mooted a scheme to hire a plane from Eastern Europe to fly directly to Shannon, and thus not touch UK soil, to pick up the Irish horses, but the authorities still said no. The whole of Ireland was in lockdown.

Cheltenham's insurers wanted them to postpone until April, but that would have clashed with Ireland's own NH Festival at Punchestown, and the same England/Ireland problem would have resulted.

Edward Gillespie flew into Dublin to meet his counterparts and discuss the problem. There, to his surprise, even the shops in Dublin's Grafton Street all had disinfectant trays at their doors. That was the extent to which Ireland went to prevent the dreaded disease reaching it. He also discovered the feelings of the typical Irishman in the street when one, recognising him as the man from Cheltenham spat out, 'Feck you up.'

Feelings were also running high near the course. Edward Gillespie tells of the mystery surrounding a number of sheep found wandering up the railway line adjacent to the racecourse. [This is the Gloucestershire Warwickshire volunteer-operated heritage steam railway, running from Toddington to the racecourse; it is used for every Cheltenham meeting, and for tourist trips. It used to be part of the Great Western Railway mainline between Birmingham and Cheltenham, via Stratford-upon-Avon.]

How the sheep came to be on the line was never ascertained, but it is probably significant that local farmers were very against the Festival going ahead.

'The local farmers all fell out with us, because we appeared to be persisting with our determination to host the Festival when, from their point of view, the countryside was closed.' says Edward Gillespie, 'We had to go on a retrieval mission and rebuild the relationships.'

An April date was agreed ten days before the March Festival was due to begin. Then, two-and-a-half weeks before the new date, an outbreak within the vicinity put the course firmly into a restricted area, and it was cancelled. With no Festival that year, a few extra races were added to Sandown's end-of-season Whitbread meeting. This was a flat meeting, featuring one prestigious steeplechase over three miles five-and-a-half furlongs (now sponsored by Betfred 365). Since 2001, it has continued to hold the Celebration Chase, put on that year to compensate for the Queen Mother Champion Chase. In 2013, it became an all-jumps meeting, and it includes presentations to the season's leading rider, trainer, owner and conditional jockey.

There was one good knock-on effect for Cheltenham following the foot and mouth disease outbreak, and that was an increase in popularity of its November meeting. The Irish flooded in, to compensate for having had no Festival, and they have continued to support it ever since, so that it has now become a not-so-mini Festival in its own right.

'It was the making of the meeting,' says Edward Gillespie, who in 2000 rebranded it as The Open, after a number of different sponsors for the feature race – the Mackeson Gold Cup back in the day, and then the Murphys, and for a short while the Thomas Pink, followed by Paddy Power up until 2015; presently it is sponsored by BetVictor.

FIELDING QUESTIONS, FINDING ANSWERS

The Cheltenham executive has fielded and found answers to many surprising questions from the Irish. Back in 2002, there was a talented mare owned by JP McManus and trained by Christy Roche, called Like-A-Butterfly. The big lady was such a nervous traveller that she used to come with an equine companion, and when she arrived at Cheltenham in 2002 to contest the Supreme Novices' Hurdle, her handlers wanted the two horses to share one stable. This could not be permitted, so the executive arranged for a builder to knock a hole between two stables and overcome the problem that way.

Like-A-Butterfly duly landed the prestigious hurdle that heralds the start of the Festival, for her eighth consecutive win. She was to win twelve of her seventeen starts, including one each of Grade Ones in bumper, hurdling and steeplechasing, before retiring to stud, breeding three foals and then unfortunately dying from colic.

* * *

Time was when a total of fifty or so Irish horses would travel over for the Festival, but nowadays that number is likely to come from Willie Mullins' or Gordon Elliott's stables alone. Willie likes his horses to be able to roll in a sand ring after working, but with only one ring available for all of the visiting horses, this was clearly not going to be possible. So, with the Mullins' horses due the next day, the executive promptly built a second one, located in the middle of the gallop in the centre of the course, where visiting horses have their exercise during the days running up to the Festival. It should be noted that the Cheltenham staff find Willie Mullins very undemanding and always polite.

The Dawn Run statue, which used to be a favourite meeting place below the paddock, now shares pride of place on the concourse above the winners' enclosure with Arkle – Ireland's greatest gelding and most memorable mare together.

For horses from a small Irish stable, perhaps with less than ten in their yard, the hustle and bustle of the 160-strong stable block at Cheltenham could be a distinct disadvantage. One such trainer was James Bowe from County Kilkenny, who bred, owned and trained the phenomenal front-runner Limestone Lad each side of the new Millennium. To help him, he was allowed to house his runner with a small local trainer, Chris Coley, who had just four boxes, allowing the visitor to feel more at home and less unsettled.

Limestone Lad won a staggering 35 of his 65 races, but he only left Ireland twice, finishing second in the 2000 Stayers' Hurdle and third in the same event in 2003, which was also his last run.

FIRE AND BRIMSTONE

The Cheltenham Festival sits on the pinnacle of the NH racing tree so securely that other important venues, like Aintree, Ascot and Sandown Park, among others, can only vie for second place. It is rather like Wembley Stadium is to the Premiership, or the World Cup is to football. Cheltenham has become a self-perpetuating (but never complacent) success story.

It was not always so unassailable. Flat racing near Cheltenham took place on Nottingham Hill in 1815, and was followed three years later by another meeting on Cleeve Hill, the magnificent backdrop to today's racing in Prestbury Park. A year later, a grandstand was built, the meeting was extended to three days, and there was even a three-mile Cheltenham Gold Cup on the Flat for three-year-olds. It was won by Spectre, which could be seen as an omen for Cheltenham's future. After a successful first ten years, the racing endured much opposition.

For a decade, the races, held in conjunction with Cheltenham Carnival, flourished, with up to 50,000 people attending. The gentry held their fashionable, generous house parties, just as they do today; drinking and gambling booths and trade stalls were set up around the races, but these attracted pick-pockets and drunkards; rules, regulations and racing discipline were scant, and temptation and greed were ever present; races themselves could be rigged or horses doped, bringing the sport into disrepute.

Enter Reverend Francis Close, evangelical Anglican priest. Responsible for some six churches that were built in Cheltenham, and for both colleges of education and the grammar school being formed, as well as two teacher-training colleges which are now part of the University of Gloucester, Reverend Close also promoted infant education and Sunday schools.

He was having none of what he perceived as the devil's work, this evil horse-racing and gambling nonsense. Fire and brimstone, hell and damnation -- his firebrand fulminations went further afield than his pulpit. Fired by his convictions, a number of his congregation descended on the races in 1829, throwing bottles and rocks at the horses and their jockeys. It is said that Reverend (later Dean) Close was himself behind the arson attack later the same year that saw the grandstand burnt to the ground.

The cornerstone for Dean Close School, Cheltenham, was laid in 1884, two years after the Dean died, and was named in his memory. Today, it has past pupils linked to a Cheltenham Gold Cup winner. Back at its foundation, the headmaster had to be someone who was ordained, and any form of acting was abhorred, so no theatre was allowed. There was no chapel either, as a governor, Reverend Griffiths, wanted the pupils to attend his church nearby; a temporary chapel was built in 1909, and the current chapel was built in 1923 in memory of pupils killed in the First World War. An indoor theatre was created in 1924, and an open-air one in 1937, and in 1991, the quality Bacon Theatre was built and named after a distinguished headmaster, Christopher Bacon. It is an established cultural asset to the town.

Today, Dean Close School is a top independent school that maintains its evangelical ethos. However, far from frowning on racing, its pupils have numbered many sons and daughters of leading racing personalities, while former member of staff Chris Haslam writes racing novels. The children of past pupil Eddie Hill and his wife Charmian, Gold Cup-winning owner of National Hunt racing's greatest mare, Dawn Run, attended. In 2015, Oliver, who co-owned Dawn Run with his mother, returned to the school while he was over from Ireland for the inaugural Dawn Run Mares' Novices' Hurdle.

There has long been an Irish connection with the school – Church of Ireland pupils used to travel from Dublin to Holyhead and then by train to Cheltenham, and a previous headmaster, from 1954–68, was the Reverend Douglas Leslie Graham, a graduate of Trinity College, Dublin. It is said that Reverend Graham was never anywhere to be seen on Cheltenham race days, so times had changed by then. Trinity College, Dublin, graduates also included Brian Wilson, who continued teaching Classics into his eighties. He was also Chaplain and head of the prep school. Another from TCD was Reverend Leonard Browne.

Back to that arson attack in 1829: With the old racecourse out of commission, racing was held for the first time at Prestbury Park in 1831, still on the flat. If Dean Close could see the Festival today, there partly as a result of his alleged antics, he would surely suffer apoplexy. At this stage, the racing was not yet permanently in Prestbury. It alternated between the hill and the park for spells, until decline and further problems set in.

Meanwhile, steeplechasing was catching the popular imagination; the first Grand National had been run at Aintree in 1839, and in 1834 the first Grand Annual Steeplechase was held at Andoversford, not far from Cheltenham. But in 1853, Prestbury Park was sold for £19,600, and the new owner was opposed to racing. He would not allow it on his land, and in 1855 it ceased. In 1881, with racing generally losing popularity, Prestbury Park was again sold, this time to Mr WA Baring Bingham, a racing enthusiast who wanted to revive its former glories. However, to begin with, he used the Park as a stud farm. It was not until 1898 that a race meeting was held there again, with some success, re-establishing racing at its current location after a gap of more than forty years.

Four years later, Prestbury Park staged a foretaste of the National Hunt Festival (9–10 April 1902). The four mile National Hunt Chase for amateur riders began in 1860. It had rotating venues, including Prestbury Park in 1904 and 1905, and it finally settled there in 1911, the first year of the NH Festival. This race is still for amateur riders over a distance of four miles, making it the Festival's longest race, and is held on the opening day. There was a new stand for that first Festival in 1911 and, small, quaint, but remembered fondly, it was to stay in commission for the next seventy years.

Between 1908 and 1934, Frederick Cathcart was both clerk of the course and chairman. He decided that as Newmarket was to flat racing, so Cheltenham should become for National Hunt, and much of the Festival's success today goes back to his groundwork. The Cathcart Chase, named in his honour, was run from 1938 until 2004, when it was superseded by the Festival Trophy (the Ryanair Chase).

Prestbury Park's chequered history was not yet quite over, for in the 1960s, its future again appeared in danger, this time from developers.

Johnny Henderson, father of trainer Nicky, wanted to safeguard its future, and that of the Festival. He, along with other Jockey Club members, formed the Racecourse Holdings Trust, and raised £240,000 to purchase the venue for posterity. The Cheltenham Festival is now safely established as the world's premier horse racing event for jumpers.

The Grand Annual is the oldest race in the NH calendar, and it now brings down the curtain on the Festival as the Johnny Henderson Grand Annual Handicap Steeplechase, run over two miles, but it is the Gold Cup that takes precedence.

CHAPTER 2

PEOPLE,
PARTIES AND
PERSONALITIES;
PUNTERS AND
PRIESTS

Cheltenham means different traditions for different people, on either side of the water, and even across 'the Pond', be it meeting up with friends, partying, betting, admiring the horses or simply savouring Cheltenham's unique atmosphere.

Two Irish-American friends stick to a particular Cheltenham ritual every year. After flying in from New York, they make their way to Prestbury Park, and then head directly for Arkle – no, not the Arkle bar, but the Arkle statue

– and there they pay homage to the greatest steeplechaser by touching the bronze model of Himself. Businessmen Niall Reilly and Aidan Shiels are not strangers to winning at the Cheltenham Festival either. In 2013, their Tony Martin-trained Benefficient was expertly ridden by then-twenty-year-old Bryan Cooper to win the two-and-a-half-mile Jewson (Golden Miller) Novices' Chase, beating Dynaste.

For Curragh-based farrier Sean Bell, punting means being at Cheltenham, usually for his annual holiday. Any celebrations will wait until the betting business of the day is concluded – and then he is likely to join in with his mates. Apart from being a holiday for him, it also means staying with family members in Lambourn. Then it is back to shoeing for flat trainer Kevin Prendergast, stud owner Derek Veitch in Rhode, County Offaly, and others, including the occasional hunter.

For many people, Cheltenham means house parties, after a day either at the Festival or watching it at home in front of the television.

For Jessica Harrington, it is staying with close friend, arch rival and nine times Festival champion trainer Nicky Henderson, at his Seven Barrows, Lambourn, training establishment. He has broken all Cheltenham Festival records, but Jessica has had some outstanding winners too – with the amazing Champion Chaser Moscow Flyer at the turn of the century; with Jezki, the 2014 Champion Hurdler; and in 2017, memorably, she became the Festival's all-time leading female trainer.

Although many of Nicky Henderson's record fifty-three Festival winners have been English- or French-bred, a number have been born in Ireland, including 2013 Gold Cup winner Bobs Worth.

Two Irish jockeys have also recorded the most Festival winners for the Seven Barrows maestro, with Barry Geraghty on fourteen and Mick Fitzgerald on ten. Mick is now well known as a TV racing presenter. Overall leading jockey at the Cheltenham Festival is Ruby Walsh, by a country mile. After the 2017 meeting, he is on fifty-six, twenty clear of compatriot Barry Geraghty.

For Valerie Cooper, widow of Irish bloodstock agent Tom, and who was herself a long-time steward in Irish racing, the Cheltenham Festival means staying with Cath Walwyn, widow of the late, great trainer Fulke, in Lambourn. She well remembers the feeling of shock in the Walwyns' house the year their fine Mill House was beaten by Arkle in the Gold Cup. Gutted Fulke may have been, but he simply got on with the next day's work.

When Magda Dunlop (nee Browne-Clayton) moved to Cashel House, Connemara, from her childhood home of Browne's Hill in County Carlow around 1950, she remembers her parents disappearing off to Cheltenham every March. 'The tickets were bought from a Mr Tully; everyone in Ireland seemed to buy their Cheltenham tickets from him.' It was travel agent Frank Tully who bought Browne's Hill House to save it from demolition through another bidder, and it remained his family home.

Hunting with the Carlow Hunt as a child before the move to Connemara, Magda remembers a redoubtable Master, Mrs Olive Hall of Ducketts Grove, who used to ride side-saddle, not in a habit but in breeches, and who regularly joined the Royal family at Windsor for visits to various events. Her son-in-law was Hardy Eustace Duckett, who Magda Dunlop remembers as tall and thin. His family name was later to lend itself to dual Champion Hurdle winner Hardy Eustace.

Brian Dunlop, Magda's late husband from Oughterard, was uncle to Mouse Morris and godfather to his and Shanny (now Bolger's) son Christopher (Tiffer), who tragically died from carbon monoxide poisoning in May 2015 while travelling in Argentina.

> For others, Cheltenham means a trip to the local bookmaker and a different type of atmosphere. Gone are the days of the smoke-filled fug, but a certain air still pervades. It will be ninety-five percent men, and they will be perched on stools, studying the form, placing their bets at the counter, and then watching where their money goes on one of the numerous televisions arrayed around the room.

MUSIC AND MERRIMENT

For Irish music duo Foster and Allen – popular worldwide for their mix of Irish traditional and folk songs – Cheltenham holds special memories, not only of the runner they had there in the 1992 Stayers' Hurdle, but also for the song they recorded for the Injured Jockeys Fund, and promoted at the Festival a decade later.

Mick Foster and Tony Allen hail from Mullingar and Moate respectively, in County Westmeath, and have been performing on accordion and guitar for forty years. They have regularly toured Australia, New Zealand, South Africa, America and Canada in addition to the UK and Ireland, but when at home, Mick likes nothing more than to ride and care for his horse, and follow the racing.

Mick Foster has been to the Cheltenham Festival many times, and in 1992 he and Tony Allen had a runner in the Stayers' Hurdle. This was a mare by The Parson which the duo bought at the last Derby Sales to be held in Ballsbridge, Dublin, in 1988. They named her Nancy Myles, after a song written by a friend, Kevin Sheerin. In later years, they discovered a pub in Tralee called the Nancy Myles, and asked the barman how it came to be named. The barman told them 'after a horse owned by Foster and Allen', without realising who he was talking to.

After her purchase, the duo asked Francis Flood at Grangecon, County Wicklow, to train her. She proved every rookie owner's dream, for she won an incredible nineteen races – three on the flat, three 'bumpers', three chases and ten hurdle races, including three at Listed level, between 1989 and 1993. She was almost always ridden by a member of the Flood family, although Mick Kinane was on board for one of her flat race wins. Her visit to Cheltenham was not so successful, as she finished down the field on what was to be her only venture out of Ireland.

Mick and Tony went on to own a number of horses, most of whom won for them – all except the horse named Foster and Allen. Another mare, the best she could manage was one second placing and three thirds.

Recording a song for the IJF was the brainchild of a friend, Seamus O'Connor, whose father Nicky was travelling head lad to Tom Dreaper during the heady Arkle days. Nicky looked after stars like Straight Fort and Carvills Hill himself, and would depart on the Sunday of Festival week with four or five runners, so Cheltenham was very much part of growing up for Seamus. He longed to go there himself, and when he was older he became a regular visitor to the Festival. In particular, he remembers standing at the last fence of the 1986 Gold Cup.

'I thought Dawn Run had no chance of getting up to win from where she was.'

He was not alone; tens of thousands more in the stands and watching on television thought the same thing, and no matter how many times the recording is replayed, you still think 'she *can't* get up.'

Seamus combines a love of music with the pub trade, and is based in Willesden, northwest London, where he quite often gets asked to recommend a sports star for opening a pub, or similar event.

It was when fellow Irishman Adrian Maguire, one of the most talented of NH jockeys, was forced to retire through serious injury in 2002, that Seamus came up with the idea of making a recording for the Injured Jockeys Fund, specifically to help people like Adrian.

He called in the willing services of Foster and Allen, and roped in a choir made up of top Irish-born jockeys AP (now Sir Anthony) McCoy, Ruby Walsh, Seamus Durak, Mick Fitzgerald, Johnny Kavanaugh, Jimmy McCarthy, Eddie Ahern, Liam Cummins, Micky Fenton, Jimmy Gallagher and Jim Culloty.

A meeting was called at the Blowing Stone pub, Kingston Lisle, close to the Berkshire Downs, where it was decided to sing 'The Fields of Athenry'. This was recorded at O'Neill's in Wardour Street, central London, directed by Richard Willoughby, currently the racing editor of the new ITV 4 Racing; at that time, he was with Racing UK, and it was their crew and cameras that were used for Seamus O'Connor's venture.

The record was promoted widely at the 2003 Cheltenham Festival, and a few weeks later a live broadcast, with the addition of Barry Geraghty in the choir, was made in the weighing room. It was shown on BBC Television at the 2003 Aintree meeting – when victory in the Grand National went to Monty's Pass, ridden by none other than Barry Geraghty, and trained in County Cork by Jimmy Mangan.

* * *

Mick Foster loves the atmosphere at the Cheltenham Festival – even though he confesses to a sneaky preference for Aintree. Like most Irish, he reveres Dawn Run, but he has more than memories of the great mare: he and Tony Allen recorded a song about her, written for them by RTÉ presenter Val Joyce, with the music by the duo's bass guitarist of the last thirty-four years, Ollie Kennedy.

Dawn Run, riding through the morning,
Striving through the icy winter's chill.
Dawn run, hooves beat out a warning,
Heart and muscles stretching up the hill.
Dawn Run, Dawn Run.

Down on a farm in County Cork
In nineteen seventy eight
A foal was born that was
To take her place among the great.

A lovely jumping pedigree,
Her story was begun
When in the racing calendar
Appeared the name Dawn Run.

Dawn Run, riding through the morning,
Striving through the icy winter's chill.
Dawn run, hooves beat out a warning,
Heart and muscles stretching up the hill.
Dawn Run, Dawn Run.

In Gorsebridge in Kilkenny
Is a trainer of renown.
At Paddy Mullins' stable
The mare soon settled down.

And in the third race of her life
At Ballybeggan Park
She won her maiden bumper.
The mare had made her mark.

After two more bumper wins
In the well-known red and black
She took to winning hurdles
With Tony on her back.

And then in nineteen eighty four
She lead them all a dance.
She won the champion hurdles
Of England, Ireland, France.

Dawn Run, riding through the morning,
Striving through the icy winter's chill.
Dawn run, hooves beat out a warning,
Heart and muscles stretching up the hill.
Dawn Run, Dawn Run.

Already in the history books
She'd found her well-earned place,
But now her next big challenge
Was to win the Steeplechase.

To Navan on a rainy day
They came from near and far
And saw what they all wanted,
A chasing super star.

A year laid up with injuries,
She threw a challenge down
And in the Durkan Brothers' race
She punched up Punchestown.

In just the fifth chase of her life
Jonjo O'Neill stood up
To ride her in the big one,
The Cheltenham Gold Cup.

She tried to run them off their feet
But couldn't quite get free
For Run And Skip enjoyed the trip
And kept her company.

She had him beaten up the hill
But danger loomed behind.
Two horses full of running,
Each with victory in mind.

I saw her beaten at the last,
At best she might be third,
But Jonjo he knew better
And said the magic word.

With bursting heart and thrusting head
She made it to the line
And Wayward Lad he knew he'd met
The greatest of all time.

Dawn Run, riding through the morning,
Striving through the icy winter's chill.
Dawn run, hooves beat out a warning,
Heart and muscles stretching up the hill.
Dawn Run, Dawn Run.

That race I will remember
In my memory of sleep.
The crowd, the cheers, the tears,
The dream, become reality.

And though we'll never see her more
Her place in history's won.
Forever Queen of Cheltenham,
That magic mare Dawn Run.

Dawn Run, riding through the morning,
Striving through the icy winter's chill.
Dawn run, hooves beat out a warning,
Heart and muscles stretching up the hill.
Dawn Run, Dawn Run.

The words were written by Val Joyce, who presented his music programme on RTÉ television for many years. Val's last show was in September 2006.

LADS' DAY OUT

Jim Sheridan is the Dublin-based, Oscar-winning film director who owned Vinnie Roe, world champion staying flat horse, who won the Irish St Leger four times and came second in the Melbourne Cup. Jim Sheridan is equally at home with NH racing, and has been to the Cheltenham Festival three times with friends. 'It was great fun,' he says.

More usually, he watches the Festival in a Dublin pub with a few mates, like Dave Kavanagh, music promoter to, among others, Celtic Woman; former punk rocker-turned-screenwriter Simon Carmody; Bono, with whom Jim often attends the Leopardstown Christmas Festival; and 'a few other lads'.

THE LADY WHO GREW UP IN GIGGINSTOWN

It is the 2017 Queen Mother Champion Chase, with nearly 58,000 spectators present, and a gentleman on the rails kindly moves back to let another lady and myself in as the runners parade. She and I begin to chat – and I discover that she used to spend all her school holidays and free time at Gigginstown, when it was owned by her aunt, Patsy Farrell, married to Johnny Farrell. Nowadays, it is the home of Michael O'Leary, his wife Anita and their four children, and it is now called Gigginstown House Stud. The maroon-and-white of his racing silks reflects Westmeath, the county where he grew up and has returned to.

The lady is Elizabeth Anne Benson, known as Dotty. She was married out of Gigginstown fifty years ago, and has lived in England for forty. Patsy Farrell was the youngest of four sisters; Dotty's mother, Sheila Kenny, was the eldest, and worked as consultant anaesthetist in the Adelaide Hospital, Dublin. Dotty did not care for city life. Her aunt Patsy was also her godmother, and they were always very close. This meant she was virtually brought up there, in the countryside around Mullingar, hunting, point-to-pointing and helping her aunt around the place. She remembers helping to clear out the house when Gigginstown was sold.

One time, after the O'Learys had bought Gigginstown, she was over in Ireland for a family reunion and Michael O'Leary invited them all for tea and champagne, and a tour of the house and gardens.

The house has had two wings added to it, but Dotty was greatly impressed with the restoration of the three- or four-acre walled garden, which had been let go in the later years of her family's involvement.

'Now it is beautifully restocked, with a fountain in the centre and paths. Michael O'Leary was very generous to us.'

Dotty is involved in racing in a minor way, having a 'leg' (one-tenth to be precise) in Raven's Tower, with Ben Pauling. The Faithful Friends syndicate were willing to pay £16–17,000 for a horse, but acquired the Darley-bred, Sheikh Hamdan bin Mohammed Al Maktoum-owned horse entire for £2,000. He was gelded, and then won three hurdles and two chases, as well as placing many times for the Faithful Friends.

2017 was the first experience of the Festival for a young Queen's Hotel intern from Switzerland. The hotel is set in the heart of the gracious town, and has long been known for partying and jollifications during race week. The young man had come across fourth-of-July celebrations before, but that occasion 'had nothing' on Cheltenham week. 'This was so much more,' he says. 'The foyer became like a night club.'

The ballroom, off to the side of the foyer and reception desk, was also full, and the Gold Cup Bar was teeming. It was an atmosphere he is unlikely to forget and, should he stay where he is, will experience again.

Michael Dickinson, who so memorably trained the first five horses home in the 1983 Gold Cup, has been resident in the USA for many years.

Responding to a letter in the *Daily Racing Form* in 2003, Michael enlightened readers about the Cheltenham Festival:

'… there is more money bet in England and Ireland on the Cheltenham Gold Cup than there is in all of America in all eight Breeders' Cup races combined … The Irish arrive in droves and add much to the electric atmosphere, and they bet like real men. The so-called World Cup of Steeplechasing provides spectacular and exciting racing, enhanced by very brave and skilled jockeys …

'When I last visited the meeting three years ago, I took my American guest to the unsaddling enclosure. He was pleasantly surprised by the huge reception given to one particular horse, to which my reply was, "That's only the fourth horse, wait until the winner comes in."

'Cheltenham is truly a memorable event for all who attend and that is why so many make a pilgrimage to the Festival every year.'

BEER, BANTER AND BONHOMIE
– ALL FOR A GOOD CAUSE

There are men in huddles, men alone and groups of men, some 200 of them, heads bent low, studying the betting sheet provided that gives current odds on the leading horses in the major races, a free pint clasped in one hand and a free betting slip in the other. One alone is wearing a tie, and he appears to spend much of the time asleep. Most sit at round tables covered in white tablecloths; a few prop up the bar. On a table in one corner are two women, also studying the form. The girl from Paddy Power, who will be taking notes in preparation for her role at a similar event next week, and the author bring the total to four women.

Many in the audience have been to the Festival before; some are looking forward to their first visit; and others will watch from betting shops or in front of their televisions at home. All are hoping to glean some worthwhile tips this evening.

The event is held in February 2017, at the Sallynoggin Inn near Dún Laoghaire, and it is the first time proprietor George Davis has hosted one. The format is similar to other such events – with a panel of experts, an MC and a betting shop representative, and the whole occasion being in aid of a charity. In this instance, it is for the Blackrock Hospice, and the €10-per-head entry fees will go to this worthy cause; the panel is sponsored by local businesses.

The evening has been organised by Liam Metcalfe on behalf of the Hospice, helped by Nial Redmond and Rory Campbell, in conjunction with George. Liam says, 'We are a group of friends who regularly raise much needed funds for the Blackrock Hospice.

'Unfortunately, one of our dear friends, Paul "Flexy" Flanagan, passed away two years ago in the loving care of the Blackrock Hospice. We were so touched by the care, devotion and compassion they showed for our friend that we decided to fundraise for them as a token of our appreciation.

'We're making the annual pilgrimage to Prestbury Park again this year, a group of eight avid racing fans, three hardened professionals with about twenty-five festivals between us, and the rest a mixture of mildly interested horse-racing enthusiasts and a couple just coming along to soak up the atmosphere.

'We're staying in a small, quaint village called Tetbury, around twenty miles from the course.'

The panellists walk up to the dais. MC Hugh Cahill introduces jockeys Andrew McNamara and Davy Russell, trainer Shark Hanlon, racing writer Donn McClean and a representative from Paddy Power, Rob Catterson. It is he who will be called upon during the evening to make adjustments to the various odds on offer for that evening only. For some he does, for others it's more than his life's worth.

Asked by Des Cahill if he still gets as excited now as he did when he first went to Cheltenham, Davy Russell replies, 'I don't get involved too much, when it hits me is when I land at the airport and pick up the signs for Cheltenham.'

Discussing the Champion Hurdle prospects, Davy Russell voices the feeling of many at the disappointment that neither of the two previous holders, Faugheen or Annie Power, will be present.

Andy McNamara pitches in with, 'Either Douvan or Altior [Arkle Novices' Chase] would romp up in the Champion Hurdle.'

The audience is busy note-taking, and there is much banter among the panellists during the evening, the main mission of which is to give betting tips to fans from experts in the know, and for the on-hand bookmaker to offer betting incentives.

Melon is all the rage for the opening Supreme Novices' Hurdle. Shark Hanlon says connections (Willie Mullins/Ruby Walsh) think that he's 'a machine'.

The Paddy Power representative notes, sagely as it turns out, that is it twenty-five years since a horse won the Supreme off just one previous hurdle run.

Regarding the Arkle Novices' Chase, Davy Russell agrees with the world in general that Altior is exceptional, but notes that Yorkhill is exceptional value at 7-1.

'He's very keen, but he'll be able to be more fluent and settle at this speed.'

The Queen Mother Champion Chase, Donn McClean declares, will be a race for watching (rather than betting on).

'It is unbelievable what Douvan can do,' he says.

Davy Russell tells the audience that odds of 1-3 on Douvan for the Queen Mother Champion Chase are brilliant. A show of hands reveals that eighty percent would back him if his price was 4-6.

The audience have had a good evening. How many of the tips will win at the Festival remains to be seen, but one certain winner is the Blackrock Hospice, for whom €2,000 has been raised.

Liam Metcalfe says, 'The Hospice has a huge shortfall in funding, mainly because of government cutbacks, and it is heavily dependent on fundraising from the public. We have organised two events in memory of Flexy on his anniversary in September, and have raised 12,000 and 8,000 euro respectively.'

They began organising their trip back in May: air tickets from Dublin to Bristol; tickets for the first three days of Cheltenham (they plan to watch Friday's sport, including the Gold Cup, from the Bell Inn in Stow-on-the-Wold); tickets for the Cheltenham Preview Night on the eve of the Festival in the Hollow Bottom Pub at Guiting Power; an eight-seater mini-bus; and a house at the Great Tythe Barn at Folly Farm, Tetbury. This is mainly a wedding venue, but for Cheltenham, the lads have rented the largest cottage available so that they can all stay together.

March has arrived, the Festival is in full swing, and the Dublin eight are in top form. Tasks are shared out: Liam and Ger are good cooks; Keith does the ironing. All of them muck in, talking about their wins or losses of the day and the prospects for the morrow. After their day at the races, they have dinner booked at a different place each evening, not too far from their base, and then it's beer, banter and bonhomie; lots of slagging and general craic.

Most of the eight know each other from school days in Dún Laoghaire. They married and moved, but this week brings them together again every year.

Nial Redmond, a Dublin postman, says, 'First and foremost it is the racing that we love.'

Liam Metcalfe, an RAC patrolman in Dublin, adds, 'And the atmosphere.'

Rory Campbell, a Weatherglaze salesman in County Wicklow, finds the English–Irish rivalry exciting. He adds, 'We have all been friends for years, and this is one way we can get together.'

'Cheltenham wouldn't be the same without the Irish,' says hospital manager Keith Neville from Dun Laoghaire. 'I love the build-up, and it's a great way of keeping in touch with old friends. At school, we played football together, but now it's the racing.' In fact, in 1980, they formed a football club called Rock United.

Gerard Hennelly, a surgical assistant in Dún Laoghaire, says, 'We don't see each other from one year to another.'

'It's the friendship,' adds Gary Thornton, a factory manager in Dublin.

Liam says, 'We used to meet up in Ireland to watch. We took the week away in places like Wexford or Kilkenny, then we decided to make the trip over.'

Hubert (Hughie) Kane, a retired Dublin postman, is 'the father of us all'. 'I've been going to Cheltenham off and on longer than Willie Mullins,' he says – nineteen times in all, starting in 1981, when he remembers Drumlargan winning the Sun Alliance (now Supreme) Novices' Hurdle in a tight finish, in which both riders, Tommy Ryan on Drumlargan and Joe Byrne, received bans of three months for excessive use of the whip.

'There was uproar over it; Joe was Irish champion at the time. But my greatest moment was watching Desert Orchid win. And Dawn Run, of course,' remembers Hughie.

Drumlargan, incidentally, trained by Eddie O'Grady, went on to win the 1983 Whitbread Gold Cup (now the Bet365) Chase at Sandown, but when he returned to hunter-chasing after a long gap, he downed tools.

Memories are part of the trip. For Liam it is having seen Kauto Star and Denman, as well as Hurricane Fly.

The friends ring home to their wives and families every day – only Liam's son, Paul, an accounts manager in London, is not married.

It has been a meeting to savour. Liam comes up with some interesting thoughts on the Festival: 'The recent changes to the layout made for an overall better experience, and there was more room to move around. It was a great week for the Irish – nineteen wins will surely never be equalled – and Cheltenham has a unique, unrivalled atmosphere.

'There are very few sporting events where fans, competitors and owners can mingle as one and shake hands and wish each other well in victory and defeat.'

He expounds some interesting thoughts on betting, too: 'I found it fascinating this year, watching all my friends each morning busy on their laptops and iPads, doing their bets for the day after breakfast. The betting world is changing, and the on-course bookmaker is in danger of becoming extinct. Why would you bet with an on-course bookmaker, when there are so many concessions and money-back offers online?'

He notes, 'All of the charity bets by the so-called experts bit the dust. The one certainty at Cheltenham is that there are no certainties, Douvan proved that. Anyway, planning for next year already.'

'THERE ARE NO LOSERS AT CHELTENHAM'

When John Seymour from County Tipperary was asked by the press about the success of Royal Frolic in the 1976 Gold Cup, he told them, 'He is probably the best horse I have ever bred at Bawn.'

His tongue was firmly in his cheek, for the stunning dark brown with a white blaze was the *only* foal he ever bred there. What's more, he had bought the mare in foal, and sold the colt on very soon after he was born.

Both the seller of the dam and then the buyer of her foal was a Tipperary veterinary surgeon, Robert John (Jack) Powell, generally known as Ginger. His son, Charles Powell, remembers, 'He wouldn't have paid big money for the foal. The colt was quite precocious, but a lovely horse to deal with, and he knew he was good. He won the thoroughbred yearling championship at Dublin Show.'

He was bought as an unbroken store horse by Fred Rimell for owner Sir Edmund Hanmer, and he was only seven when he won NH racing's Blue Riband in 1976, ridden by Irishman John Burke from County Meath. A few weeks later, John Burke also won the Grand National at Aintree on Rag Trade, but in 1995, he died from a heart attack at just forty-one years old.

Charles Powell remembers his own first visit to the Festival clearly, as it was 1965, when Arkle won the second of his three Gold Cups. At the time, he was pupil assistant to Toby Balding.

'Cheltenham is the Mecca, and my parents used to go every year when I was stuck at school, so 1965 was very special for me. It was a fantastic first visit. Pat Taaffe had ridden for my parents, and Tom Dreaper was a friend of theirs. Seeing Arkle win was one of those things you dwell on.'

Apart from his father's connection with Royal Frolic, his uncle, Jim Powell, also produced Kerstin as a youngster. A brown mare born at Shanbally Stud, Tipperary, she was sold to England (like so many in those days), and went on to win the 1958 Gold Cup, the second of only four mares to have won it to date.

Charles Powell says, 'It's easy to become a pub bore when you have even a slight relationship with Gold Cup winners. It's an achievement for horses, jockeys and trainers just to get to Cheltenham, and they make it so special for the Irish.

'I've never had a runner there, but I have friends who have, and it's great to support them. There are no losers at Cheltenham, because to have a horse good enough to get there is a feat in itself. Part of the atmosphere is people walking up and congratulating others. To witness a good horse coming up the hill is sheer joy.'

He adds, 'Istabraq was a racing machine.'

Charles Powell's brother, John, a vet like his father, is senior steward of the Irish National Hunt Steeplechase Committee (INHSC), and is credited with bringing the Turf Club and the INHSC together as custodians of the integrity services in Irish racing. But he is more than that: a week after qualifying as a vet in 1971, he had an accident that left him a paraplegic, but he never allowed that to interfere or impede with his work, says his brother. 'He has set the bar very high for any future aspirant.'

Charles Powell and his partner Jane Hodges seldom miss a Cheltenham Festival. They love it. Charles also enjoys coming out with sayings, such as, 'Fools and foals meet at the sales,' and, 'Happier they who ride for their own pleasure and not to astonish others.'

> Two Irishmen chatting outside a Dublin pub during one of the numerous Cheltenham preview evenings.
>
> 'Have you ever been to Cheltenham?' asks one.
>
> 'Yes, twice,' says the other. 'Once to the races and once to prison.'

PRAYING AND PARTYING

Cheltenham used to be associated with shamrocks and priests, but both have dwindled in recent years. There was a time when Irish priests were forbidden from racing, but, come Cheltenham time, it was surprising how many of them 'had to attend a course'.

The best known was Father Sean Breen, who never missed a Festival in forty years from Arkle's first Gold Cup in 1964; he died in 2009, at the age of seventy-two. His last parish was Ballymore Eustace, County Kildare.

Father Breen – 'the Breener' – is remembered for the well-attended Mass he would give outside a Cheltenham hotel each year before the Festival, as well as for his tips. It was he who, in 2005, blessed Kicking King shortly before that horse won the Gold Cup for trainer Tom Taaffe.

Father Breen was also a successful racehorse owner, and formed the Heavenly Syndicate with two friends. Their flat horse, One Won One, won twelve races, trained by Joanna Morgan, a friend of his (and who has joined the ranks of trainers to give up). Father Breen was also co-owner of Portant Fella, which won fifteen races under NH rules. Unfortunately, he did not live to see a Joanna Morgan-trained runner at the 2009 Festival called Raise Your Heart. Another horse, trained by Oliver Sherwood, was named after him – The Breener won the Challow Hurdle at Newbury, and finished third in the Supreme Novices' Hurdle at the Festival.

He said part of the fun of Cheltenham was catching up with old friends. He raised many hearts and souls, and is quoted as saying, 'There is nothing in the Bible that says you can't gamble. We have to lighten up a bit.'

For Father Jimmy Browne, priest in residence for Ballyneale and Grangemockler in County Tipperary, the fun with friends is at home around the television for big races like the Gold Cup, with plenty of food and drink on hand. 'It makes a nice finish to the hunting season, and a nice social gathering,' he says.

He adds that he doesn't go to Cheltenham, because he is not good in crowds, 'but I'm okay in a pen of cattle or horses'.

Of priests at Cheltenham, he says, 'That generation has almost died out. The sporting tradition doesn't exist among the younger priests. There's very few sporting clergy left; they don't hunt, shoot, fish or have a dog.'

CHAPTER 3

THE RACES

So, what is it that draws these thousands to Cheltenham each year? First, there are the principal races, that have led to the Festival being known as the Olympics of National Hunt racing – or, indeed, the World Cup.

THE CHELTENHAM GOLD CUP

The Cheltenham Gold Cup is the Blue Riband of Steeplechasing, but when it began, in 1924, it played second fiddle to the Grand National at Aintree. That mighty race, however, is a handicap, where the Gold Cup is run off level weights. It is thus a level playing field, leaving the way for truly the best horse to win (there has been a weight allowance for mares since 1984). In a handicap, the best horse may carry as much as two stones (12.7kg) more than horses of inferior ability.

The first Gold Cup carried prize money of £685, and was won by Red Splash, ridden by Dick Rees and trained by Fred Withington, after whom a four-mile one-furlong chase that used to be run at Cheltenham's New Year's Day card was named. The prize fund for the 2017 Gold Cup was £575,000, of which £250,585 went to the winner.

The second running of the Gold Cup, in 1925, produced the first Irish-trained winner, in Ballinode, trained by Frank Morgan and ridden by Ted Leader. She was the first of four mares ever to have won the race, followed by Irish-bred Kerstin in 1958, and two Irish-trained mares, Glencaraig Lady in 1972 for Francis Flood and jockey Frank Berry (now racing manager to JP McManus) and Dawn Run in 1986 (Paddy Mullins/Jonjo O'Neill). Ireland has always had a healthy handful of Gold Cup winners, as we shall see.

* * *

Prince Regent set the Tom Dreaper Cheltenham ball rolling after the Second World War, winning the 1946 Gold Cup. By then aged eleven, many have speculated on how many more he would have won had racing at Cheltenham not been cancelled during the War. For some years into Arkle's mighty reign, Tom Dreaper himself still considered Prince Regent the better.

Luck brought the son of My Prince to him, because after breaking him in for owner Jimmy Rank, Prince Regent was due to leave Dreaper to be trained in England. However, the intended trainer, Gwynn Evans at Druid's Lodge near Stonehenge, died. The outbreak of the Second World War put paid to any other plans to bring him over, and so the horse stayed in County Meath, and won many races, including the 1942 Irish Grand National. The 1946 Cheltenham Gold Cup saw him start at odds of 4-7, and in the race, he swept his five opponents aside one by one and drew clear to win impressively.

Prince Regent was ridden by a true horseman of the era, Tim Hyde, who, in 1953, was to have a silly little fall in a local show-jumping class that broke his back and left him paralysed for life. He trained from a wheelchair, but during his riding career he won the Cheltenham Gold

Cup on Prince Regent, the 1939 Grand National on Workman and the 1938 Irish Grand National on Clare County.

* * *

Only two years after Prince Regent, it was Ireland's turn again. This time the trainer was the then-little-known Vincent O'Brien, aged thirty-one, from deep in County Tipperary. It was the start of an extraordinary period for Vincent O'Brien, that brought him a total of twenty-three Festival wins, including four Gold Cups, three Champion Hurdles and an amazing ten Gloucestershire Hurdles. This race is now known as the Supreme Novices, and it is the curtain raiser of the Festival. Over the years, it has thrown up dozens of future stars, many of them trained in Ireland. The genius young Vincent O'Brien then turned his hand to flat racing, with phenomenal success. He died in 2009, at the age of ninety-two. He will never be forgotten on either side of the Irish Sea.

Cottage Rake was not a big horse, but he etched his name on the Gold Cup in three successive years: 1948, 1949 and 1950.

Aubrey Brabazon rode him to all three of his Gold Cup victories, at 10-1 in 1948, and odds of 4-6 the next year, by which time the public appreciated his qualities; he was still odds on in 1950, at 5-6.

Both horse and jockey reached iconic status, and are remembered indelibly in the lines:

Aubrey's up, the money's down,

The frightened bookies quake.

Come on, me lads, and give a cheer,

Begod 'tis Cottage Rake!

The Brabazons have a long heritage of racing in Ireland, from before Aubrey up until the present day, but it is Aubrey, whose life revolved around the Curragh, who will always be remembered best.

* * *

Knock Hard gave Vincent O'Brien yet another Cheltenham Gold Cup, before he turned his finely tuned brain and horseman's hands to flat racing. Knock Hard fell in the 1952 Gold Cup, but in 1953, ridden by Tim Molony of another great Irish racing family, he put up an exceptional performance to win for owner Moya Keogh.

Tim Molony also won four Champion Hurdles, the first with Hatton's Grace in 1951, followed by three consecutively on Sir Ken, trained in England by Willie Stephenson. In later years, Molony bought an Irish-bred yearling for 400 guineas at Goffs Sales – this was none other than Red Rum, later an immortal Grand National hero. Molony died in 1989, aged seventy. His equally talented brother, Martin, won the 1951 Cheltenham Gold Cup riding Silver Fame, a horse which still holds the record for the most wins at Prestbury Park. Martin Molony died in July 2017, aged ninety-one. The brothers hailed from County Limerick, where Martin's son Peter runs the successful Rathmore Stud.

* * *

Six years after Knock Hard, the Irish won the Gold Cup again in 1959, with the Danny Morgan-trained Roddy Owen, on ground that resembled a quagmire. Some might call it lucky, as, of the three ahead of him at the last fence, Pas Seul fell and nearly brought down Linwell, who in turn badly hampered Lochroe. Pas Seul made amends in 1960.

Roddy Owen was ridden by Bobby Beasley, who was to win the Gold Cup fifteen years later on Captain Christy, having been 'to hell and back' during the interim due to a drink problem. It was hugely to his credit that he made such a comeback.

Roddy Owen's trainer, Danny Morgan, had himself won the Gold Cup in 1938, riding Morse Code, the only horse ever to beat Golden Miller at Cheltenham.

* * *

How to sum up Arkle in a few words? He was simply the best. His superiority was boundless, and he had character to match. He knew he was king, and would stand imperiously at a paddock entrance before deigning to walk in, as if he were an actor checking he had the full attention of his audience. Many words have been written about 'Himself', as Arkle became known in Ireland, but there are always more gems to unearth, and for those lucky enough to have been around in his day, the memories remain forever.

His full story can be read elsewhere [*Arkle: The Legend of 'Himself'*, The O'Brien Press], but suffice to say he won the Cheltenham Gold Cup three times in succession, from 1964 to 1966, always ridden by Pat Taaffe, and trained by the quiet genius Tom Dreaper. His 1964 win, when he beat Mill House, was in record time.

He was beaten in only four steeplechases. The first time was when he slipped at Newbury in the 1963 Hennessy Gold Cup, the only time Mill House got the better of him; the last time was when he broke a pedal bone in the King George at Kempton on Boxing Day. In between, he was twice beaten shouldering welterweights, once at the Cheltenham December meeting for the Massey Ferguson Gold Cup (carrying 12 stone 10lbs), and once in the Hennessy Gold Cup at Newbury, when Stan Mellor rode a superbly canny race to beat him on Stalbridge Colonist. The rest of his steeplechasing career included winning the 1962 Honeybourne Chase by twenty lengths at the Cheltenham November meeting, now called The Open; and the Broadway Chase (now the RSA Chase) at the 1963 Festival. He then took the next three Gold Cups, 1964–66, twice beating Mill House, and in 1966, the year when he ploughed through the last fence at the end of the first circuit, he beat Dormant. Ironically, this was the horse who passed the lame Arkle in Arkle's last race when he broke his pedal bone.

After rest and recuperation from his injury, Arkle came back into training, and in fact was one day off returning to the racetrack. But Pat Taaffe dismounted after working him, and told Tom Dreaper that the 'feel', the magic, wasn't there. Wisely, time was called. There was to be no ignominious downhill slide for him, as one can think of for such as Cottage Rake, Flyingbolt and others. Sadly, he did not make old bones, as arthritis got the better of him in 1970, aged thirteen.

* * *

Just two years after Arkle's third Gold Cup, in 1968 Tom Dreaper and Pat Taaffe won it again, this time with the ten-year-old Fort Leney, owned by John Thomson. This was a much closer finish than Arkle ever had in the Gold Cup – but who knows what the result might have been had not Mill House uncharacteristically fallen at the last open ditch?

The Big Horse, as Mill House was affectionately known, was Irish-bred and initially raced there, but was sold to be trained in England, where he won the 1963 Gold Cup as a precocious six-year-old. In 1964 and 1965, he met with defeat at the hands of Arkle, and did not take on the great horse in 1966. Now here he was, in 1968, with no Arkle in the race, only to fall.

Stalbridge Colonist almost fell at the second last when poised to challenge, which left Fort Leney and The Laird battling it out, with the inimitable Peter O'Sullevan calling, 'It's between England and Ireland now.' Fort Leney just got the better of the scrap by a neck, and Stalbridge Colonist was closing fast, finishing only one length behind.

* * *

The 1970s were golden years for Ireland in the Gold Cup, winning it in 1970, '71, '72, '74, '75 and '77.

Golden Miller, bred in County Meath and trained in England in the 1930s, won five Gold Cups and a Grand National. The closest any other horse has got to that was L'Escargot, but unlike 'The Miller', he did not win his National in the same season as either of his Gold Cups. In fact, it was four years later when he had slid quite a way down the handicap, and had already twice placed, having at his first attempt taken a dislike to Aintree. It was Tommy Carberry, who died in July 2017, who cajoled him around.

L'Escargot was a 'quirky' horse – that is, he had a mind of his own, but he was brilliantly ridden by Tommy Carberry and trained by a master at his game, Dan Moore. Dan Moore had been a champion jockey, and was once beaten a short head in the Grand National, before the days of a photo finish. The race was adjudged to go to little Battleship and 17-year-old Bruce Hobbs, but Dan Moore always felt he was the winner with Royal Danielli.

Dan Moore, a bit like Vincent O'Brien, made Cheltenham his stamping ground, and he trained thirteen Festival winners.

The first time L'Escargot won the Gold Cup, in 1970, he started at odds of 33-1. He beat another Irish horse, French Tan, and the fast-finishing Spanish Steps, one of several NH stars bred by Edward Courage in Oxfordshire. French Tan was ridden by Pat Taaffe, and the pair outjumped L'Escargot at both the last two fences, but Dan Moore's charge showed in front at the post.

Having seen that L'Escargot was no snail, punters ensured that in 1971 he started at odds of 7-2. He beat Tom Dreaper's novice Leap Frog, also 7-2, by a healthy ten lengths, with The Dikler another fifteen lengths back in third. The Dikler's turn was to come two years later, when he beat Pendil by a head.

L'Escargot was owned by American Raymond Guest, former Ambassador to Ireland and a great racing enthusiast under both codes. He won the Epsom Derby twice in the 1960s, with Larkspur and Sir Ivor, before adding the Cheltenham Gold Cup and the Grand National. Both his Derby winners were trained by Vincent O'Brien, who had long since left Cheltenham behind to train Classic winners.

* * *

The mare Glencaraig Lady was trained by Francis Flood in Grangecon, County Wicklow, and ridden by Frank Berry, now racing manager to JP McManus.

The Dikler was back trying again in 1972, and so was Spanish Steps, along with the great Australian horse Crisp, whose next race was to be his unforgettable effort in the Grand National. The clear leader and superlative jumper fatigued in the dying strides to let in Irish-bred Red Rum, on his first National foray.

Glencaraig Lady was close to the inside rail and stalking the Gold Cup leaders, The Dikler, L'Escargot, Crisp and Royal Toss. Frank Berry brought the mare with a superbly timed run to take the spoils in a photo finish.

Frank Berry rode for Francis Flood for eighteen years, and was among the first to pay tribute to him when he died in October 2016, aged eighty-six.

'Winning on Glencaraig Lady was great for me. It was my first ride at Cheltenham as well. It was a huge occasion. … We had a lot of good years together. He was a wonderful man to ride for and he was just a nice man,' he told the *Irish Independent*.

Bred by Patrick Doyle, Glencaraig Lady was an unusual winner not only for being a mare, but also because she was twelve years old.

* * *

Pat Taaffe and Cheltenham went well together. He added another Cheltenham Gold Cup triumph in 1974, this time as a trainer, in a dramatic race.

As they swept down the hill on the last circuit, five horses were in close contention, but the picture changed when High Ken fell at the notorious third from home, and brought down Pendil. As the remaining three headed for home, the Queen Mother's Game Spirit was left behind, and The Dikler and Captain Christy went head-for-head.

The novice Captain Christy, ridden by the comeback king Bobby Beasley, jumped the second-last superbly and took a slight advantage. He blundered at the last fence and The Dikler took over, but the younger legs of Captain Christy prevailed for a popular Irish winner.

* * *

In 1975, the colours made so famous and adored by Arkle added another Gold Cup for Anne, Duchess of Westminster. Ten Up was trained by Tom Dreaper's capable son Jim, and ridden by Tommy Carberry. His main challenger in the race was Bula, who was trying to make history as the first horse to win both the Champion Hurdle and the Gold Cup; that accolade would have to wait more than a decade, as a mistake at the last left Bula unable to use his speed against Ten Up, who stayed every yard of the stiff three miles two furlongs. As Ten Up swept to victory, Soothsayer snatched second from Bula.

In later years, the Duchess gave Ten Up to a godson of hers, James Hodges from Hampshire, and he won a number of military races on the old boy.

* * *

One of Ireland's characters is Mick O'Toole, and in 1977 he added the Gold Cup to his impressive CV with Davy Lad, owned by Anne-Marie McGowan and ridden by Dessie Hughes. Davy Lad won the 1975 Sun Alliance Novices' Hurdle at the Festival, and the next year he finished unplaced in the Sun Alliance Novice Chase, won by Tied Cottage.

But another year on, in the Gold Cup, everything was different. Tied Cottage characteristically led the Cheltenham field, but Somerville overtook him sweeping down the hill, with Davy Lad tucked in behind. Coming to the last fence, Dessie slipped through between the other two, Davy Lad put in an extravagant jump at the end of three stiff miles, and the pair swept to victory.

* * *

Always trained by Paddy Mullins, but bred, owned and in the early days ridden by Mrs Charmian Hill, Dawn Run was indisputably NH's greatest mare. She is the only horse ever to have won both the Champion Hurdle and the Cheltenham Gold Cup. In 1984, she won the English, Irish and French Champion Hurdles. In 1985, she won her first steeplechase in Navan, beating Buck House and Dark Ivy. A slight tendon injury put her out for a year, which meant that when she came back in 1986, she could not run in novice company. Two more steeplechase wins in Ireland preceded her unseating Tony Mullins in the January trials meeting in Cheltenham.

This meant that when she lined up for the Gold Cup, with Jonjo O'Neill in the saddle, she had just four steeplechases behind her. In the race, she set out to make all the running, but was headed at the last by Wayward Prince and Forgive'n Forget. Third was now the best spectators could hope for. But in one of the most emotional and spectacular finishes up that infamous slope, she responded to Jonjo's galvanisation, dug deep and, in extraordinary fashion, produced the 'impossible' and won going away.

She fell at the first next time out in Aintree – she was very 'buzzed up', which may have been a reaction to excited scenes in the Cheltenham unsaddling enclosure. She then won a private match race against the Champion Chase winner, Buck House, at Punchestown; and then headed for France in June. There, on a blazing hot day, she missed out a jump five from the finish, fell and broke her neck.

Two of her lifetime rivals, Buck House and Dark Ivy, both also died that spring, Buck House from colic, and Dark Ivy broke his neck at Becher's in the Grand National. Desert Orchid, meanwhile, whom Dawn Run beat on every occasion they met, including the Champion Hurdle, went on to a long and illustrious career, which included winning the Cheltenham Gold Cup of 1989 and four 'King Georges'. He lived to the ripe old age of twenty-six, and was one of the most beloved steeplechasers on either side of the Irish Sea.

* * *

It was to be a decade before the next Irish-trained winner of the Gold Cup. Imperial Call was trained in County Cork by Fergie Sutherland. The brown gelding, bred by TA O'Donnell and owned by Lisselan Farms Ltd, won the 1996 Hennessy at Leopardstown impressively from reigning Gold Cup holder Master Oats. This resulted in Imperial Call becoming his trainer's first Cheltenham Festival runner. There, ridden by regular jockey Conor O'Dwyer, Imperial Call beat Rough Quest, who, just over two weeks later, won the Grand National at Aintree. The popular grey One Man was favourite, and the future Queen Mother Champion Chase winner threatened two out. He didn't see out the trip, and clambered over the last fence to fade. Imperial Call, meanwhile, lived up to his name, jumped imperiously and galloped all the way to the line.

Imperial Call came up against many of the well-remembered horses of his day. Early on, he was beaten a short head by Doran's Pride in a hurdle race; nearly five years later, he was to beat him in the John Durkan

Memorial Chase at Punchestown. Danoli was a much-loved Irish horse who beat Imperial Call into third in the Hennessy Cognac Gold Cup at Leopardstown. Imperial Call also beat Florida Pearl on his penultimate start, in the Heineken Gold Cup at the 1999 Punchestown Festival.

Imperial Call won twelve of his twenty-four chases, placing in a further seven, and won four of his eight hurdle races.

'Fergie' Sutherland was brought up in England and Scotland, was taught to ride in Somerset by royal trainer Dick Hern, attended Eton College and Sandhurst, joined the 5th Inniskilling Dragoon Guards, and lost a leg in the Korean War. He set about acquiring different prosthetic legs according to activity, such as riding, shooting or dancing.

He trained initially in England, and numbered a Royal Ascot winner among his successes. It was only when he heard that his mother, Joan, was planning to sell Aghinagh House in Killinardrish in 1967 that he moved over to County Cork. Converting the farm outbuildings to some of the best racing stables in Ireland, he set about training there with considerable success, including Go Go Gallant, Tempo and Pancho's Tango; he also bought young horses to make and sell on.

A much-loved character on the racing scene and beyond, he died in 2012, at the age of eighty-one.

* * *

Into the 2000s – and the Millennium winner was the Irish-bred Looks Like Trouble, for Irish-born trainer Noel Chance. There was no Festival in 2001, due to foot and mouth disease (see page 18), and then came the reign of Best Mate. Bred in County Meath, he won for three consecutive years, from 2002 to 2004, for trainer Henrietta Knight, with Kerryman Jim Culloty in the saddle every time.

2005 brought the first Irish-trained victor in the new Millennium, with the Tom Taaffe-trained Kicking King. It was the era of the Celtic Tiger, and Kicking King's owner Conor Clarkson was a successful developer during that time. Tom Taaffe was his natural choice of trainer, as the two were (and are) friends, and Conor already had a number of horses with him.

Tom Taaffe, son of Arkle's legendary rider Pat, was a top jockey in his own right, and won on every single racecourse in Ireland. Just as Dan Moore had given Pat Taaffe his first ride as a jockey, so his son Arthur Moore did the same for Tom Taaffe.

Of Kicking King's owner, Tom Taaffe told me shortly after the race, 'He has a great passion for racing, and his best attribute is he's as good a loser as he is a winner.'

Kicking King is a bright bay by Oscar, bred by Sunnyhill Stud at Kilcullen, County Kildare.

Kicking King showed enough promise to be entered in the principal races at Cheltenham. He was second in the 2003 Supreme Novices' Hurdle to Back In Front, and second again to Well Chief in the 2004 Arkle Challenge Trophy Novices' Chase.

He saved his best for the most important one of all – the 2005 Gold Cup. Before it, Tom's wife Elaine asked Father Sean Breen to attend their stables at Straffan, County Kildare, to give Kicking King a blessing.

He went in to Cheltenham off the back of three wins and a third (to Beef Or Salmon at Down Royal). His win in the King George at Kempton on Boxing Day was somewhat hair-raising: he was ten lengths clear at the last, but blundered badly, and Barry Geraghty performed like a limpet to stay in the saddle.

Luckily, he made no such mistake in the Gold Cup where, in a fifteen-runner field, he took a strong hold, settled down and then ran on strongly to beat 25-1 shot Take A Stand by five lengths.

In the next season's King George, re-routed to Sandown, Kicking King beat Monkerhostin by a neck, but unfortunately tore a tendon. He was off the racecourse for just over two years, and placed second or third in three of his remaining five races.

Kicking King was ridden in all twenty-six of his races over jumps by Barry Geraghty, and is now among the elite retired racehorses at the Irish National Stud in Kildare, who visitors can admire in their paddocks.

* * *

The following year, 2006, Ireland won again, with War of Attrition. His story is told on page 124.

* * *

Irish-bred Imperial Commander, winner of the 2010 Gold Cup, ridden by Paddy Brennan, does not go down as an Irish winner, as he was trained in England by Nigel Twiston-Davies. By Flemensfirth, he retired to Mount Top Stud, County Antrim, and in 2017, at only sixteen years old, died of a heart attack in the field. He was a Cheltenham specialist, winning six races there, including the 2006 Bumper and the 2009 Ryanair Chase. His Gold Cup win over Denman and Kauto Star in 2010 was as high a point as it is possible to attain. Kauto Star was odds-on, but was not on his best form that day, and eventually fell four out. In the resulting two-horse finish, Imperial

Commander proved stronger than the great Denman, and won going away. It was more than twenty lengths back to 50-1 shot Mon Mome in third, who the previous year had won the Grand National at 100-1.

For jockey Paddy Brennan, it was the ultimate dream. A native of County Galway, he moved to England in 2000, and was champion conditional jockey in 2004–05. In 2016, he joined the elite band of jump jockeys to have ridden 1,000 winners.

Imperial Commander's bunch of owners, Our Friends In The North, will certainly never forget their horse. One of them, Ian Robinson, said after his death, 'That day at Cheltenham, he wrote his own great chapter in his own words when he wasn't part of the narrative of the race … He was exceptional, and took us to places we could never dream of. We just hung on to his tail on the wonderful journey.'

Mount Top Stud was where Imperial Commander had spent his summer holidays and pre-training each year. He had been taking part in showing classes in his retirement, and was due to parade at Punchestown during the 2017 Irish NH Festival later that month.

* * *

Although Lord Windermere was a shock winner in 2014, no trainer deserved it more. Jim Culloty, a native of County Kerry who now trains in County Cork, is most remembered for his association with Irish-bred triple winner of the Gold Cup, Best Mate. He also won the Grand National in 2002 on Bindaree, just after the first of Best Mate's Gold Cups. His win as a trainer, with Lord Windermere, put him in that select group of jockeys-turned-trainers who have both ridden and trained a Gold Cup winner.

It is hard for a new trainer to get going, though a Gold Cup win will boost any trainer's profile. Nevertheless, like a number of others, Jim Culloty finds the going tough.

Lord Windermere, owned by Dr Ronan Lambe, has won twice at the Festival – he took the 2013 RSA Novices' Chase on the back of one win in a beginners' chase and three places. But his Gold Cup win of 2014 was more of a surprise, because in his three previous runs that year, his form read eighth, seventh and sixth. Nevertheless, ridden as in the previous Festival by Davy Russell, he showed great tenacity at the moment that mattered, to beat On His Own by a short head. Earlier in the race, he had been nearly tailed off.

Neither he nor long-time leader Silviano Conti kept a true line on the run-in, and afterwards a Stewards Enquiry was held to decide whether the race should be awarded to On His Own; they decided not to alter the placings. It was a sweet victory for Davy Russell, who shortly before the Festival had been sacked by Gigginstown House Stud, for whom he was retained jockey, in favour of rising star Bryan Cooper, himself sacked three years later.

Lord Windermere, by Oscar, lost his form and pulled up behind Coneygree in the 2015 Gold Cup. He looked back on track in early 2017, when narrowly beaten first time out, and in the Grand National he was a staying-on seventh.

* * *

Don Cossack is, of course, Gordon Elliott's most special horse, his pride and joy. German-bred, on his first outing in a bumper Don Cossack played up at the start and finished an immature fifth, but for the rest of his career he was a model of consistency, and was placed every time that he stood up. He did have the occasional jumping lapses, which led to three falls.

He won three bumpers under Nina Carberry; his first maiden hurdle, ridden by Davy Russel; and his first beginners chase for Andrew Lynch. He fell on his first visit to Cheltenham in the 2014 RSA Chase, and the following year he was third in the Ryanair Chase – not an auspicious start to his Festival forays. On his next outing, in the 2015 Melling Chase at Aintree, he won, beating the consistent top-drawer horse Cue Card. The tables were turned when Don Cossack fell two out behind Cue Card in the King George VI Chase at Kempton on Boxing Day.

The scene was set for the 2016 Gold Cup, for which Don Cossack was favourite, ahead of Cue Card. There were other good names in the nine-horse field, including Djakadam, who had been second behind Coneygree the year before, Don Poli and the grey, Smad Place. As they approached the tricky downhill fence three out, Cue Card joined leaders Don Cossack and Djakadam, but crumpled on landing. Approaching the last fence, Don Cossack held the lead and ran on powerfully to score – to the roar of the Irish, as the first four horses came from across the water. Djakadam was second again, Don Poli third, and County Waterford trainer John Keily's Carlingford Loch came in fourth. Second and third were both trained by Willie Mullins.

The result was a dream come true for Gordon Elliott, and plenty of celebrations followed. For the second time, a Gigginstown horse paraded through the streets of Mullingar, Michael O'Leary's home town, following War Of Attrition's Gold Cup in 2006.

Don Cossack, a dark brown with a white blaze, acquired a slight tendon injury and is now retired, but in the spring of 2017 he was still in residence at Cullentra, County Meath, and enjoying admiration from visitors. He was also swimming every day and taking gentle exercise on the horse walker. His retirement will be at Gigginstown.

Secretary Zoe Winston sums up the Gold Cup-winning day with one word: 'surreal.'

Ireland won the Gold Cup again in 2017, and the story of Sizing John's victory is told on page 228.

THE QUEEN MOTHER CHAMPION CHASE

The Champion Chase began life in 1959, taking the place of a race that would not feature at a place like Cheltenham today. This was the National Hunt Juvenile Chase for four-year-olds, and was staged from the inaugural Festival in 1911 up until 1958, when the last winner was the appropriately named Bee Off, ridden by amateur John Lawrence (later Lord Oaksey).

Ireland won the first three stagings of the Champion Chase, which is run over the minimum distance of two miles and therefore produces steeplechasing at its fastest and most exciting.

First up was Dan Moore, who won with Quita Que, ridden by Bunny Cox. Dan Moore's son Arthur was to win it in 1981 with Drumgora, ridden by Frank Berry. Tom Dreaper won the next two after Quita Que with Fortria, ridden by Pat Taaffe, in 1960 and 1961.

This was the great Tom Dreaper era, and he added more Irish success with Ben Stack in 1964, and two years later with Flyingbolt, still considered by many to be the only horse to come close to equalling Arkle. Tom Dreaper added two more in 1969, with Muir (the only one of his not ridden by Pat Taaffe, but Ben Hannon) and Straight Fort in 1970. It was Dan Moore again in 1973, with the Tommy Carberry-ridden Inkslinger. Two years later it was Tom Dreaper's son Jim who showed his training skills, producing Lough Inagh to win in the hands of Sean Barker, for many years a part of the Dreaper setup at Greenogue, County Meath.

The Irish were on a roll, winning the next four as well, with Skymas in 1976 and '77, trained by Brian Lusk and ridden by the inimitable Mouse Morris. In 1978 and '79, it was the turn of the Peter McCreery-trained Hilly Way, ridden the first year by Tommy Carmody. In 1979, he was ridden to victory by Ted Walsh, to date the only amateur to have won the race.

Two more Champion Chase winners came Ireland's way in the 1980s, with Drumlargan in 1981 and Buck House in 1986. It was in 1980 that the Queen Mother prefix was added to the race in honour of the Her Majesty, who was eighty that year.

The decades of numerous Irish wins reduced, with just one in the 1990s, ten years after the last one, when Arthur Moore won it again. This time it was with Klairon Davis, ridden by Francis Woods, whose father, Paddy, used to be Arkle's work rider, and won his only race on the great horse.

Into the new Millennium, and the age of Moscow Flyer, winner in 2003 and 2005, followed by New Mill, 2006; Big Zeb, 2010, Sizing Europe, 2011, and Special Tiara, 2017, the last two both trained by Henry de Bromhead.

* * *

Newmill's story: By the time horses contest the Queen Mother Champion Chase, they usually have considerable experience, and so generally there is no more than the occasional faller. But the 2006 race was packed with drama, resulting in half the field of twelve coming home riderless. It began right at the first fence, where a French contestant unshipped his rider.

The great Kauto Star was favourite, but he fell at the third, and brought down another. Two more lost their jockeys four out, and another one went at the second-last fence. With the exception of Kauto Star, these were all outsiders. Meanwhile, one horse –Newmill – led from the first and stayed there, away from the trouble.

Jockey Andrew McNamara gave the eight-year-old a superb ride, and won by nine lengths, drawing away from the AP McCoy-ridden Fota Island and 50-1 shot Mister McGoldrick.

Irish horses filled the final three places, with Central House in fourth for trainer Dessie Hughes and jockey Roger Loughran; old former dual-Queen Mother winner Moscow Flyer (Barry Geraghty), who retired after this race (see page 108); and finally, Watson Lake for trainer Noel Meade and jockey Paul Carberry.

Newmill was led up that day by his regular work rider, James Dullea, who was on a learning curve towards eventually getting his own training licence.

Of course, many considered Newmill simply a lucky winner. The following month, however, at the Punchestown Festival, he franked the form by winning the Irish equivalent, the Kerrygold Champion Chase, beating Fota Island again, even more easily.

In Newmill's early career, which included winning the Goffs Land Rover bumper and the Grade 1 Royal Bond Novices' Hurdle at Fairyhouse, he was trained by Thomas O'Leary. In his Champion Chase heyday, he was with another Cork trainer, John Joseph Murphy, and in his old age, he was trained by James Dullea.

By Norwich, his breeding on the dam's side was closely related to Gold Cup winner The Dikler. His breeder was Veronica O'Farrell, and his owner Mary Hayes.

He was a top-level hurdler, but an even better chaser. He went into the Champion Chase fresh from winning the Kinloch Brae Chase at Thurles, and it was greatly to his credit that in older age, with his best form well gone, he won the race again in 2010 as a twelve-year-old.

> The Irish loved the Queen Mother, and she presented the trophy for the Champion Chase right up until she was one hundred years old. One year, an Irish owner kissed her, Edward Gillespie recalls, and said, 'May you live for a thousand years.' She died aged 101.

THE CHAMPION HURDLE

More than any other of the Championship races in the twenty-first century, the Irish have made the Champion Hurdle their own. Between 2001 and 2017, they have won it nine times, and three times immediately before that through Istabraq. They have been big players in its sponsorship, too. Commercial sponsorship of the Champion Hurdle began in 1978, initially backed by the now sadly defunct Waterford Crystal. Smurfit/Smurfit Kappa began supporting the race in 1991, and from 2010 it has been sponsored by UK betting company Stan James.com.

Introduced in 1927, the Champion Hurdle was won in 1928 by the Irish-bred Brown Jack, one of his seven wins from ten starts over hurdles, but his destiny lay elsewhere. His trainer, Aubrey Hastings, died and Brown Jack went to Ivor Anthony, for whom he become immortalised as one of the most popular and best staying flat racers ever. He made the two-miles five-furlongs Queen Alexandra Stakes at Royal Ascot his own, winning it for six years running, from 1929 to 1934.

In 2008, the Wednesday of Cheltenham was postponed due to high winds that had devastated temporary structures. The gale had abated by mid-morning, leaving an air of serenity, but the damage was done and, on the advice of the structural engineers in charge of the marquees and other temporary structures, and of the Police, there was no choice but to postpone racing. The scheduled races were relocated to the Thursday and Friday. There was an unexpected local bonus, because on the Wednesday, with no racing to attend, Cheltenham town was flooded with visitors; the local shops and pubs had never seen such trade.

Although Vincent O'Brien is thought of as 'father' of the Irish at Cheltenham, there was one Irish-trained winner of the Champion Hurdle before O'Brien's three-timer with Hatton's Grace. This was Distel in 1946, trained by Charles Rogers for the eccentric Brit Dorothy Paget, and ridden by Bobby O'Ryan. Miss Paget, daughter of Lord Queenborough, bought Ballymacoll Stud in County Meath in 1946, and installed Charlie Rogers as manager. She never visited it herself. Although principally a flat-racing stud, it was also the birthplace of Arkle in 1957. After Miss Paget's death, it was sold in 1960 to Michael Sobell and Arnold Weinstock. In July 2017, the stud was sold at auction for €8.15 million, and appears set to continue as a world-class enterprise, with a majority of mares descended from the founding mares.

Charlie Rogers, whom Miss Paget dubbed her 'Romeo', was one of few trainers who could handle the notoriously difficult owner, and he saddled three winners for her at the 1946 Cheltenham Festival.

* * *

Vincent O'Brien, like Charlie Rogers, was a founding member of the Irish Racehorse Trainers Association in 1950. This was in the midst of his Cheltenham Festival heyday when Hatton's Grace graced the Champion Hurdle scene, winning from 1949 to 1951, the last at the ripe old age for a hurdler of eleven. Owned by Mrs Harry Keogh, Hatton's Grace was ridden to his first two Champion Hurdle victories by Aubrey 'The Brab' Brabazon, and in 1951 by Tim Molony.

After his incredible NH career, funded initially through successful betting, Vincent O'Brien turned his deft hands to flat racing, and was leading Irish trainer thirteen times between 1959 and 1989. He was also twice British champion both on the flat and in jumping, and he trained the winners of twenty-seven Irish Classics, sixteen in England, twenty-five Royal Ascot winners and, as already noted, twenty-three winners at the Cheltenham Festival.

* * *

It was not until 1960 that the next Irish-trained winner of the Champion Hurdle appeared, and this was Another Flash, trained by Paddy Sleator, ridden by Bobby Beasley and owned by John Byrne.

Paddy Sleator was an accomplished amateur rider, and won the Champion Irish amateur title three times – in 1934, 1937 and 1938. He was leading Irish trainer in 1958, on prize money won, and saddled the highest number of winners consecutively from 1955 to 1961. The 1960 Champion Hurdle with Another Flash was the highlight of his Cheltenham Festival winners. He was as good at training flat winners, and won the Irish Cesarewitch three times.

* * *

In 1963, Alan Lillingston became the first of only two amateur riders – both of them Irish – ever to have won the Champion Hurdle, riding the one-eyed Winning Fair for George Spencer, father of leading flat jockey Jamie. George Spencer also owned the eight-year-old gelding.

There were twenty-one runners, and Winning Fair put three lengths between himself and the runner-up, Farney Fox, with Quelle Chance a neck away in third.

Alan Lillingston became a Turf Club Steward and Secretary of the National Hunt Committee. He was also an international dressage and eventing rider, which he turned to after breaking his neck racing. He also rode as an amateur for Tom Dreaper, notably having started Flyingbolt off to a successful career in a bumper at Navan.

Alan Lillingston ran the successful Mount Coote Stud in Kilmallock, County Limerick, and died in 2014, aged seventy-nine.

The only other amateur-ridden Champion Hurdler was For Auction, steered to a 40-1 victory by Colin Magnier in 1982. The Michael Cunningham-trained six-year-old was owned by Danno Heaslip. Two flights out, six horses were almost in line, but it was the outsider who stamped his authority on the event, drawing clear on the run to the line. His amateur jockey looked like a professional in the saddle, giving the horse a masterly ride.

It was to be another fifteen years before Ireland's next Champion Hurdle win, but it heralded a rich era: Monksfield toughed it out to win it for trainer Des McDonagh and owner Dr Michael Mangan in both 1978, ridden by Tommy Kinane, and 1979, ridden by Dessie Hughes.

Sea Pigeon was runner-up both times, but his turn came in the following two years – and after that, it was Ireland again.

When Tommy Kinane won the Champion Hurdle on Monksfield he was forty-five years old, an age by which the majority of jump jockeys have long since hung up their boots. Not the teak-tough Tommy. He had ridden at the Festival before, including in the Champion Chase, but not in the Champion Hurdle. Rather than walk the course, he ran round it, perhaps to prove his fitness.

Like many other Irishmen, he lodged with ex-pat family members in England. In his case, it was with relations in Middlesex, travelling by coach to Cheltenham along with his family and his kit, and stopping for breakfast at the Puesdown Inn at Compton Abdale, near Cheltenham.

As an octogenarian, he remembered the race well: 'I wanted to make use of his stamina. I knew the others [Sea Pigeon and dual winner Night Nurse] would be queuing up behind, ready to pounce. I needed to get first run, and so I set sail for home.

'We flew down the hill, soared over the second last, and were clear so tight on the rail that no-one could have got up our inside.'

Speed, adrenalin and race-craft were like a drug. He had the best possible ally in Monksfield, and together they galloped towards the final flight. Sea Pigeon, ridden by Frank Berry, was pressing them, but Monksfield put in a superb winning leap and landed running. With only that hill ahead of him, the issue was put beyond doubt. It was the crowning moment in the veteran jockey's long career.

The next year, connections opted for a younger man, and it was the mild-mannered Dessie Hughes who steered Monksfield to a second successive Champion Hurdle, again beating Sea Pigeon.

Monksfield was a full horse, and went on to sire a number of winners, one of which, Ross Venture, won ten NH races.

* * *

Little did we know it then, but Dawn Run's 1984 Champion Hurdle was just a foretaste of what was to come. It was the first year that a mare's allowance of 5lbs had been introduced, and she took full advantage of it.

In 1983, ridden by Ron Barry, she had finished second in the Sun Alliance Novices' Hurdle. Now, with six wins under her belt in the year since then, she was odds-on for the Champion Hurdle.

During that period, she had also been beaten into a fast finishing second to the reigning Champion Hurdler, Gaye Brief, at Liverpool, only one day after winning a handicap hurdle at the same venue on her next appearance after the Sun Alliance. Even then, she turned out again to win the Novices' Champion Hurdle at Ireland's NH Festival at Punchestown.

Now, lined up against her in the Champion Hurdle were her nearest market rival in the betting, one Desert Orchid; the 1982 Champion, For Auction; Very Promising and Buck House, and nine others. In the event, it was one of these outsiders, the Jim Old-trained Cima, a 66-1 shot, who gave her most to-do. But tenacity was one of Dawn Run's key trademarks. Her victory, by three-quarters of a length, was achieved in record time.

The story of how Dawn Run was in danger of losing the race, due to the scrimmage around her in the unsaddling enclosure, is told on page 177.

* * *

Istabraq was a three-times winner of the Champion Hurdle, in 1998, 1999 and 2000 – and had not the 2001 meeting been abandoned due to the outbreak of foot and mouth disease, a record-breaking fourth victory was widely expected. He became one of Ireland's best-loved and most revered horses.

There is also the sentimental side to it, for the classicly-bred horse, who did not live up to expectations on the flat, was spotted by John Durkan, who hailed from Stepaside, south of Dublin, while he was working for UK trainer John Gosden.

John Durkan was a young man, about to embark on his training career. He had achieved ninety-three wins as an amateur rider, and had been assistant trainer in top stables in England. He was sure that if he could begin his career with a horse of this class, it would get him off to a good start, and he set about persuading JP McManus to buy Istabraq for him to train. He achieved this, had Istabraq gelded, liked what he saw and dreamed the dream. Then he fell ill. A certain young Aidan O'Brien was called upon to train him, just until John got better. But he did not. He was struck down with leukaemia, and listened to Istabraq's 1997 win over Mighty Moss in the Sun Alliance Novices' Hurdle from a New York hospital bed, where he was to have a bone marrow transplant the next day. He died in January 1998, aged thirty-one, just two months before Istabraq won his first Champion Hurdle – but John knew by then that the horse was going to fulfil his potential.

This was massive. Istabraq won twenty-three of his twenty-nine hurdle races, came second three times (one of these by a short head on his hurdling debut), fell twice in his penultimate season, and pulled up in his final race, a fourth attempt at the Champion Hurdle in 2002. Charlie Swan rode him in every single one of his hurdle races.

He won his first Champion Hurdle by an easy twelve lengths over Theatre World at 3-1. It was the last time he was to start at odds-against until his final run, some seventeen races and four years later.

In the 1999 Champion Hurdle, he beat Theatre World again, and in 2000 it was Hors La Loir who came off second best. He was to win two years later in the hands of his regular Irish jockey, Dean Gallagher. These are the bare bones of one of Ireland's greatest equine athletes, and it is fitting that he took the Irish from the last century at Cheltenham into the current one.

THE STAYERS' HURDLE

Although there have been only two Irish-trained winners of the Stayers' Hurdle in the current century – the ultra-game Solwhit in 2013, and Nichols Canyon in 2017 – it was not always this way. Nine winners were Irish-trained in the two decades from 1975 to 1995.

A long-distance hurdle has nearly always been a feature of the Cheltenham Festival, but to begin with, in 1912, the year after the Festival was founded, it was a lowly-selling hurdle. The winner's connections won £100 in prize money, and the winner, Aftermath, was sold for £50 in the post-race auction. The following year, the prize money was doubled. The Stayers' Selling Hurdle lasted until 1938, bar a gap of two years between1928 and 1930, and a further two lost to weather. Silver Bay (1913 and 1914), Warwick (1923 and 1925) and Sobrino (1930 and 1933) were all dual winners. There was also a selling chase at the Festival from 1923 to 1942 (shock, horror, there would be no such race at the world's premier jump meeting today).

The Spa Hurdle, better remembered these days as part of Cheltenham's New Year's Day meeting, was run at the Festival over three miles, once in 1923 and again in 1942. It then became a regular stayers' festival feature from 1946 to 1967, and was run just once again in 1971. Winners of the Spa Hurdle include the 1955 Champion Hurdler Clair Soleil, who won it four years later ridden by Fred Winter. Merry Deal won it aged twelve in 1962, five years after winning the Champion Hurdle. Beau Normand, trained by Bob Turnell, is the only dual winner, having been successful in 1963 and 1967.

From 1972, it morphed into its modern guise as the Stayers' Hurdle, sponsored by Lloyds Bank and, from 1978, by Waterford Crystal. The sponsor from 1991 to 2004 was Bonusprint.

It is only since the Festival was extended to four days in 2005 that the race has been elevated to Championship status, and the feature of the third day, Thursday. With that, and new sponsors Ladbrokes, its name was changed to the World Hurdle. Ladbrokes pulled out before the 2016 renewal, and Ryanair stepped in for a year, adding it to their feature race, the Ryanair Chase over two miles five furlongs on the same card and of the same value.

2017 brought a new sponsor, Sun Bets, and a reversion to its original name of the Stayers' Hurdle. Eleven of the winners between 2000 and 2016 have been ridden by Irish jockeys.

* * *

When Solwhit won the World (Stayers') Hurdle in 2013, it was a victory for the 'ordinary' men who owned him, the four members of the Top Of The Hill Syndicate, as well as trainer Charles Byrnes.

As with Brave Inca in the 2006 Champion Hurdle, it showed that not only fabulously wealthy owners win at Cheltenham. Brave Inca was owned by two Wexford men and their five sons. Solwhit was owned by four men, also from County Wexford: Thomas Power from Kilmore, former amateur rider Pat O'Hanlon, Hugh Martin who runs a supermarket in Enniscorthy, and publican Ger Gaynor.

They told the *New Ross Standard* after their win that 'We had a quiet enough night on Thursday. There's no point in throwing our money around over there; we said we'd wait till we got home.'

Instead, celebrations continued long into the night when they got back on Irish soil. 'From Gaynor's pub to the Newtown Road, and Clonagaddy, Kilmore Village to Tomnalossett, Enniscorthy, the roofs were raised when the Charles Byrnes-trained nine-year-old got the better of Celestial Halo to surge up hill and claim the prize that for so long has belonged to the side-lined Big Bucks.'

Fast enough to win on the flat, Solwhit's two-mile hurdling career was blighted by Hurricane Fly, also born in 2004. He was beaten four times by him, including by a neck in the Punchestown Champion Hurdle at the 2010 Irish NH Festival, but Solwhit was one of only a handful to turn the tables on 'the Fly'. He achieved this in the Punchestown Hurdle of November 2009.

Although thereafter always beaten by him, Solwhit was well placed by County Limerick trainer Charles Byrnes, and Solwhit's top-class CV included twice winning the Grade 1 Aintree Hurdle, in 2009 and four years later in 2013, his next run after winning the World Hurdle.

He missed just short of two years through injury, from after a race in January 2011 until he next appeared in December 2012. Just two runs later, and attempting three miles for the first time, he triumphed in the World Hurdle at Cheltenham. It was also a training triumph, as well as one of the greatest of many great rides by now retired jockey Paul Carberry.

Outside of his highlight Cheltenham win, possibly the race of Solwhit's life was when he beat Punjabi by a short head in the 2009 Punchestown Champion Hurdle. Punjabi had won the Champion Hurdle at Cheltenham the previous month. Throughout his career, Solwhit was a real trier, and it was exceptionally bad luck that in the autumn of 2014, contesting a schooling hurdle at Thurles, he fell and broke his shoulder.

Charles Byrne told the *Racing Post,* 'He was an unbelievable horse for me. I wouldn't even know where to start. He has taken me to places I never would have dreamed of going. I've never had anything like him before and probably won't again.'

RYANAIR CHASE (FESTIVAL TROPHY)

The Festival Chase was sponsored by *The Daily Telegraph* in its inaugural year of 2005, but has been sponsored by Ryanair ever since, by which name it is universally known. It was promoted to Grade 1 status in 2008. The race was designed to give a chance to horses not fast enough for the Queen Mother Champion Chase, but who did not stay the stiff three-and-a-quarter miles of the Cheltenham Gold Cup, or for those on the ladder up to the ultimate championship, and it has successfully bridged this gap.

In its thirteen runnings, eleven winners have been ridden by Irish jockeys. Past winners have included Albertas Run twice (Tony McCoy), Cue Card (Paddy Brennan) and Dynaste, but it was not until 2016 that an Irish-trained horse won, the ill-fated Vautour for Willie Mullins and Ruby Walsh. The same stable took it again in 2017 with Un De Sceaux.

There was no direct equivalent to the Ryanair Chase before its foundation, but there was a novice chase of the same distance, known at the Cathcart, open to first- and second-season chasers. Run from 1938

Above: Epitomising the very best of the Irish at Cheltenham – Arkle and Pat Taaffe.
Right: Aubrey Brabazon, who rode both Cottage Rake and Hatton's Grace, trained by Vincent O'Brien, to multiple Gold Cup and Champion Hurdle victories.
Below: The statue of Dawn Run and Jonjo O'Neill, long a popular meeting point at the Festival.

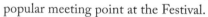

Above: Maureen Mullins, matriarch of the Mullins clan. At 87, she still adds a joyous and well-dressed touch in the winners' enclosure at Cheltenham.

Right: Highly-regarded owner JP McManus, flanked by his wife Noreen and racing manager Frank Berry.

Below: Istabraq wins the 1998 Champion Hurdle, the first of three for JP McManus and jockey Charlie Swan.

Above: Full flight – Hardy Eustace and Conor O'Dwyer in perfect harmony on their way to 2004 Champion Hurdle victory.
Below: The Guinness Village. Spot the female! This is where the queues for the gents are longer than the ladies.

Above: Kicking King powers his way up the finishing straight to win the 2005 Gold Cup under Barry Geraghty.

Below: Kicking King at home in Straffan, County Kildare, with trainer Tom Taaffe.

Above: Newmill spread-eagles his rivals to win the 2006 Champion Chase under Andrew McNamara, at odds of 16-1.
Right: This is what it's all about – the Novices Syndicate, comprising Wexford's Crean and O'Tierney fathers and sons, flank trainer Colm Murphy to celebrate the 2006 Champion Hurdle victory of (**below**) Brave Inca, ridden by Tony McCoy.

Above: War Of Attrition wins the 2006 Gold Cup for jockey Conor O'Dwyer, trainer Mouse Morris (**right**), and Gigginstown House Stud owners Michael and Eddie O'Leary (**below**), who seem to be saying, 'Shall we do it this way – or that way?' Either way is pretty successful.

Above: Sublimity survives a mistake at the last flight, to win the 2007 Champion Hurdle from former heroes, Brave Inca and Hardy Eustace.
Below: Owner Bill Hennessy and son Robbie congratulate jockey Philip Carberry.

Above: Trainer Gordon Elliott in the winners' enclosure with connections of Labaik, after he sprang a surprise to win the 2017 Supreme Novices' Hurdle under teenage jockey Jack Kennedy.

Right: St Patrick's Day at Cheltenham, and the Irish are out in force.

Below: Irish jockeys join in the fun (from left to right): Patrick Mullins, Davy Condon, Martin Ferris, Paul Carberry, Brian O'Connell, John Cullen, Alain Cawley and Robbie Power.

until 2004 (as a hunter chase for three years between 1975 and 1977), it was twice won by Dan Moore's Quita Que, in 1958 and 1961. He also won the inaugural Champion Chase in 1959. Along with the 'Ryanair' in 2005, a new novices' chase called the Jewson was founded.

Naturally, Michael O'Leary likes to have at least one runner in 'his' race, but has yet to win back his own money. He might well have done so in 2006, when his War Of Attrition was well fancied. But in the event, that horse was aimed even higher, and duly landed the Gold Cup, the ultimate prize.

ARKLE CHALLENGE TROPHY

Affectionately known as 'the Arkle', this race began life as the Cotswold Chase until 1969. It always surprised me that a two-mile race that Arkle never contested should have been chosen to bear his name instead of the three-mile Broadway Chase, which he did compete in. The Broadway is now known as the RSA, and Arkle won it as a six-year-old in 1963, the same year his future great rival Mill House won the Cheltenham Gold Cup, and at the same age.

The Cotswold, now the Arkle, has therefore thrown up many more Queen Mother champions than Gold Cup heroes (only Alverton), but they have been some of the very best.

Tom Dreaper won it five times, with Fortria in 1958, Mountcashel King in 1961, Ben Stack in 1963, Flyingbolt in 1965 and Alpheus in 1971. Ireland next took it in 1979 with Chinrullah, trained by Mick O'Toole and ridden by Dessie Hughes; Anaglogs Daughter in 1980, for Bill Durkan and Tommy Carberry; The Brockshee in 1982, Arthur Moore/Tommy Carberry; Bobsline in 1984, Francis Flood/Frank Berry; and Boreen Prince in 1985,

Andrew McNamara/Niall Madden. Ten years later, it was Arthur Moore again, with Klairon Davis (Francis Woods), 1995; and in 1996, Ventana Canyon (Edward O'Grady/Richard Dunwoody).

The first Irish winner of the new millennium was Moscow Flyer in 2002, (Jessica Harrington/Barry Geraghty) – Moscow's story is told on page 108. Tom Cooper from County Kerry trained the 2009 winner, Forpadydeplasterer, ridden by Barry Geraghty for enthusiastic owners the Goat Syndicate, named after a pub they frequented in Goatstown, south Dublin. Henry de Bromhead and jockey Andrew Lynch took the prize in 2010 with Sizing Europe (see page 111); and in both 2015 and 2016, Willie Mullins and Ruby Walsh took the prize through Un De Sceaux and Douvan.

The race had Irish sponsors for many years, beginning with Waterford Crystal and then Guinness in the 1990s, followed by the *Irish Independent* ten times in the new century.

SUPREME NOVICES' HURDLE

Since its inception in 1946, when it was known as the Gloucestershire Hurdle, Ireland has won this race an extraordinary forty-six times. Until 1972, it was always held in two divisions, bar twice, when three divisions were run: in its first year, and again in 1961.

Vincent O'Brien won it an astonishing ten times, with most of his winners being ridden by Tommy Burns, plus two by his brother Phonsie, and one by Pat Taaffe.

One of his winners in 1952 was Saffron Tartan, who went on to win the 1961 Cheltenham Gold Cup, when trained by Fred Winter.

In 1974, the race took on the title Champion Novices' Hurdle, and the mantle Supreme Novices' Hurdle followed four years later. This is also when it was moved forward to become the Festival's curtain raiser – and with it came the now familiar roar from packed, excited crowds as the tapes go up, and their money rides on the horses' backs for the next three-and-a-half to four minutes.

Throughout the years, this race has revealed a number of other future champions, such as Flyingbolt (Champion Chase), L'Escargot (two Gold Cups and a Grand National), the ill-fated Golden Cygnet in 1978, Buck House (Queen Mother Champion Chase) and in the current century the likes of Brave Inca, Vautour and Douvan.

THE CAPTAIN REMEMBERED

The name Harty is synonymous with Irish racing. Cyril Harty rode as an amateur, and was a captain in the Irish Army, also representing Ireland in show-jumping. His son Eddy won the 1967 Grand National on Highland Wedding for Toby Balding; and his son, Eddie junior, trained a winner at Cheltenham, not just with his first Festival runner but with his first runner in England. This was, appropriately, a horse named after his grandfather, Captain Cee Bee, and it came only four years after obtaining his licence at the mature age of forty-two, having previously been a banker.

The race was the 2008 Anglo Irish Bank Supreme Novices' Hurdle, sponsored by the very bank Eddie had left four years earlier. Captain Cee Bee, spotted by Eddy senior as a foal, stormed up the final hill under Robert Thornton to beat future Champion Hurdle winner Binocular, who, like Captain Cee Bee, was owned by JP McManus.

Captain Cee Bee was back at the Festival two years later, running unplaced in the 2010 Arkle Chase behind Sizing Europe. He ran again the next year, and finished third to the same horse in the Queen Mother Champion Chase.

He reverted to hurdling, via a win on the flat at the Curragh and, remarkably, he was back at Cheltenham again in 2014 for the Champion Hurdle, no less, and ran with credit to finish fifth behind Jezki.

Eddie Harty said, 'Captain Cee Bee burst blood vessels, and we felt as he got older that jumping hurdles took less out of him than chasing.'

COUNTY HANDICAP HURDLE

This used to be the last race of the Festival meeting, and as such was known as 'the get-out', with considerable wagers being laid. It has always been as well to follow the Irish, who, in the last seventy years, have had an excellent record. Irish-trained horses occupied the first six places in 2015. Three Mullins brothers have all trained winners: Tony (2007, Pedrobob), Willie (2010, Thousand Stars; 2011, Final Approach; and 2017, Arctic Fire) and Tom (2012, Alderwood).

This is the race that was chosen to bear Vincent O'Brien's name from 1995 until 2016. In 2017, it was sponsored by Randox Health. Vincent O'Brien continues to be remembered at Cheltenham as one of only twenty-five equine and human inductees in the Hall of Fame, situated inside the main entrance.

The first County Hurdle was run in 1920, and won by Trespasser, ridden by George Duller, who until 1973 also had a race named after him at the Cheltenham Festival. Ruby Walsh has been in the winning saddle four times.

In 1970, the County Hurdle victor Khan became the first winner to be trained by a woman at the Cheltenham Festival. This was Delma Harty, twin daughter of Henry Harty of Patrickswell, County Limerick.

CROSS-COUNTRY STEEPLECHASE

Another race founded in 2005, following the extension of the Festival to four days, was the Cross-Country Steeplechase, run over three-and-three-quarter miles. Although not popular initially among the press room and punters, it has an enthusiastic following, especially among the Irish and those who like to walk to the centre of the course to watch close up; for many of them, the race is a highlight.

It has established itself as a keenly contested test of riding and equine skills, and can be a good betting opportunity. It is run over a unique course of thirty-two fences inside the pukkah track, and consists of some hugely diverse fences: hedges, 'cheese wedges', 'Aintree', banks and ditches, rails and water, and it finishes with a pair of stuffed hurdles on the racecourse proper.

It is a race that Ireland, with its great tradition of riding across country, has made its own, winning eleven of the thirteen renewals. England's Balt-hazaar King won the other two; he is now retired and hunting in Wiltshire. It is a race that can reinvigorate horses, giving them different things to think about.

Racehorses that are used to hurdles or steeplechase fences have to learn to adapt to the array found here. No-one is better at this than cross-country king Enda Bolger. He has built replica cross-country fences around his training establishment in Bruree, County Limerick, so that by the time his horses come to the Cheltenham cross-country, they are well versed in the obstacles that lie ahead.

The first running of the event was won by Enda's veteran Spot Thedifference, ridden by one of the most respected Irish amateur riders, John Thomas – JT – McNamara.

Enda also trained Heads On theGround (2007), Garde Champetre (2008, 2009) and Josies Orders (2016). All four of these were ridden by cross-country queen Nina Carberry, who is from an outstanding family of County Meath cross-country riders.

Besides Enda Bolger, the other successful Irish trainers are Philip Rothwell, Michael Hourigan, Henry de Bromhead, Peter Maher (with Big Shu, from one of the smaller stables), Tony Martin and, in 2017, Gordon Elliott.

The winner in 2017 was Cause Of Causes, a feat which put him into an elite band of horses who have won three different races at the Festival. These include Arctic Gold in the 1950s, Flyingbolt in the 1960s and, in more recent times, Bobs Worth and Vautour.

The JP McManus-owned, Gordon Elliott-trained Cause Of Causes had won the Fulke Walwyn/Kim Muir in 2016, and the National Hunt Chase in 2015. He was ridden each time by Irish amateur JJ – Jamie – Codd, who has won more than 700 point-to-points in Ireland.

Afterwards, Gordon Elliott said, 'He's an absolute superstar and we love him to bits. Jamie also gave him a great ride.'

Just three weeks later, the nine-year-old Cause Of Causes and Jamie Codd finished second in the Aintree Grand National to One For Arthur.

COURAGE AND CARE

JT McNamara won more than 600 races in Ireland and England, including an incredible sixteen cross-country races at Cheltenham, one of which was at the Festival. He frequently rode for fellow Limerick man JP McManus, often on horses trained by Jonjo O'Neill or Enda Bolger.

JT's three other Festival wins include the four-mile National Hunt Chase in 2002 on Rith Dubh, by a head over the Davy Russell-ridden Timbera.

Unplaced was a horse ridden by one Mr G Elliott for Martin Pipe. The longest Festival race, the NH Chase attracts high-class runners, and the 2016 renewal was won by Minella Rocco, who twelve months later finished runner-up in the Gold Cup. JT also won the 2007 Foxhunters on Drombeag, and he was back in the National Hunt Chase winner's enclosure in 2012 on Teaforthree.

One year later, and with the decision already taken to retire at the end of the season, JT took an horrific first-fence fall on Galaxy Rock in the Fulke Walwyn/Kim Muir handicap chase for amateur riders. He was paralysed from the neck down. The whole of Ireland's racing fraternity and beyond, including the horse's owner JP McManus, pulled together to raise funds for him, his wife Caroline and their three young children, and to offer whatever practical support they could.

JT was able to return home fifteen months after the fall, but thirteen months later, in July 2016, he lost his greatest battle. Naturally, tributes poured in for the man who epitomised so much that jump racing stands for: riding ability, fitness, jockey-craft, not a little humour, determination and, above all, courage. He was forty-one.

At his funeral, Canon Gary Bluett said JT's life revolved around his passions: family and racing. 'Strong willed and determined, he had a great command of some words in the English language – some might not be found in the Oxford dictionary.'

For 2017, the National Hunt Chase was fittingly given the prefix JT McNamara. Others remembered likewise in recent years have been Sir Peter O'Sullevan, John Oaksey, Terry Biddlecombe and Toby Balding.

Ironically, in July 2013, just four months after the Cheltenham fall, and contesting the Listed Summer Plate at Market Rasen, Galaxy Rock, with AP McCoy in the saddle, again fell at the first, and was himself fatally injured.

CHAPTER 4

HEROES AND HEROINES – A FEW FAVOURITE HORSES

For many people, Cheltenham is seeing the finest horses close up, and the memories they take home with them …

PACKING A POWER PUNCH – ANNIE POWER

Few racehorses, and even fewer mares, have set the pulses pumping as much as Annie Power – and when she crashed out at the last flight when a 'street' clear in the 2015 Mares Hurdle at the Cheltenham Festival, the collective groan could surely be heard in Cheltenham town. It was one of those falls that looks horrendous, but luckily the chestnut and rider Ruby Walsh got up virtually unscathed.

Chestnuts are relatively rare these days in racehorses, where the vast majority are bay or brown. In the horse world generally, chestnut mares have long borne a reputation as hot-headed, but with a crucial caveat: a bit like the little girl with a little curl in the middle of her forehead, when she is good she is very, very good, but when she is bad she is horrid. A good chestnut mare simply doesn't give in. She will try her heart out, and will be determined to 'beat the boys'. Annie Power is one such.

Annie Power was bred by former Gaelic games All Star Eamon Cleary by a successful Irish-based German sire, Shirocco, out of useful mare Anno Luce, which he bought at the 2007 Goffs Sales carrying Annie Power. Eamon Cleary bought Anno Luce for breeding, liking the pedigree, which included classic wins in Germany from the granddam, Anna Paola. Shirocco's seven wins included the German Derby, the Coronation Cup at Epsom, beating the popular mare Ouija Board, and the Breeders' Cup Turf for owner-breeder Baron G Von Ullman and French trainer Andre Fabre. Eamon Cleary hoped the resultant foal would make a decent middle-distance flat racer, being likely to possess both speed and stamina.

He intended to put the dam, Anno Luce, back in foal, but with his chosen stallion Teofilo's book full, he sold her on. Luckily, he kept the chestnut filly foal. Born at the Hylands' Oghill House Stud, County Kildare, she was looked after by John Banaghan and then broken in by Ross O'Sullivan, before going into training at two years old with fellow GAA enthusiast Jim Bolger.

Jim Bolger found she needed time to grow and mature, so she did not race as a two-year-old; it was the same story at three. By four, Jim Bolger declared her ready. Showing real promise at home at last,

Eamon Cleary named her after his feisty grandmother, Annie Power, from a village called The Rower, in County Kilkenny.

He told a local paper that his grandmother 'was from a very well regarded family named the O'Keefes in The Rower, whose house was burned to the ground by the Black and Tans, and she resisted them. Afterwards the family had to live in hedges and on the run for a time. She was a very special woman in my life. She lived in Ballinvegga, Ballywilliam, after she was married.'

Eamon Cleary had been keeping the special name up his sleeve until he thought he had a horse worthy of it – and that he had in bucketsful, for Annie Power went through her first ten races unbeaten, starting with a Galway bumper win first time out. She was snapped up by Willie Mullins for Rich and Susannah Ricci after her second win.

Willie Mullins is on record as saying, 'I was there that day [her second race] and it was the first time I had seen her in the flesh. I can still remember this beautiful, deep-girthed filly and for her to win like that [by fifteen lengths] was deeply impressive.' (www.ownerbreeder.co.uk, Joseph Burke)

After her three bumper wins (two of them restricted to mares only), Patrick Mullins also took the ride for her first hurdle, as he was successfully chasing the amateur jockeys' title, but thereafter stable jockey Ruby Walsh was always in the saddle on the racecourse.

At home in Closutton, the County Carlow stables of Willie Mullins, her regular work rider was Jason Dear, who in his spare time loves nothing more than to ride, and often win, in local open hunter trials.

With Cheltenham 2014 approaching, Annie Power had good enough credentials to try for the Champion Hurdle, but with Hurricane Fly the stable's two-mile hurdle star, it was decided to try the mare over three miles in the World Hurdle. She met her first defeat, at the hands of More Of That; 'The Fly' meanwhile had been uncharacteristically beaten into fourth place in the Champion Hurdle.

By the time of the 2015 Cheltenham Festival, the stable faced a dilemma of riches: Ruby Walsh chose, correctly, to ride new-boy-on-the-block Faugheen over the wonderful little Hurricane Fly, on whom he had already won two of the last four Champion Hurdles, and the useful Arctic Fire was also entered. Annie Power was clearly also of Champion Hurdle calibre, but she had had only one previous run that season, due to a small injury. And so, with Faugheen in the same ownership, she was routed for the Mares' Hurdle.

It should have been a cake-walk. She was so vastly superior to her fifteen rivals that five of them started at odds of 100-1, two at 66-1, and all bar two of the others had odds in double figures. As Annie Power came into the last flight, four lengths up and drawing further away, it looked to be all over bar the shouting. But for some reason, she failed to get high enough at the flight, and fell headlong.

As horses trained by Willie Mullins and ridden by Ruby Walsh had already won three races that day – Douvan in the opening Supreme Novices' Hurdle, Un De Sceaux in the Arkle Novices' Chase and Faugheen in the Champion Hurdle – many punters, especially the Irish, had Annie Power as the fourth leg of an accumulator. Her fall was widely reported as saving the bookies a payout in the region of £50 million. (The Mullins team in fact took the first three places in the Champion Hurdle.)

So, Annie Power had been to Cheltenham twice and failed twice, the only two blemishes on her otherwise immaculate copybook.

Sweet – the sweetest – compensation was to come her way. First, she quickly got back into winning ways in the Mares' Champion Hurdle at Punchestown, Ireland's National Hunt festival, that May. She did not reappear until February 2016, following a small injury, when she easily won a mares' hurdle at Punchestown, at odds of 1-20.

Faugheen, unsurprisingly, was favourite to retain his hurdling crown, and so Annie Power was to be aimed at the Mares' Hurdle again. But then Faugheen got injured, and so did 'second string' Arctic Fire. At the last minute, and with the owners paying a £20,000 supplementary entry fee, Annie Power was re-routed, and would at last get a chance of proving herself in the most important hurdle race of all, the Champion Hurdle.

And she did it in style, against worthy rivals, leading from flag-fall to winning post in an exhibition round that brings goose pimples to watch. As if to stamp her authority, she achieved it in record time.

Three weeks later, in the Aintree Hurdle, she added a fifth Grade 1 to her record, scoring even more easily than in the Champion Hurdle, and again beating My Tent Or Yours. She was all set to defend her crown in 2017, when the news broke late in January that, having overcome one injury, she now had another, and would not be coming to Cheltenham. Only a week before, Willie Mullins had declared that she and Faugheen might well take each other on in the Champion Hurdle, which would have been a mouth-watering prospect. Instead, both were ruled out, Faugheen having also suffered a setback.

In April 2017, a week before the Irish NH festival at Punchestown, it was announced that Annie Power was confirmed in-foal to Guineas and Derby winner Camelot. She was entered for a number of races at Punchestown, and had seemed in good form until a day or two before she was due to run, and 'time' was wisely called.

Later, with the decision having been taken to retire her, Willie Mullins told the *Racing Post*, 'She was a very special racemare and gave us many memorable days. Her Champion Hurdle win last year was definitely one of the highlights of my career as a trainer.

'To see her landing running over the last in the Champion Hurdle, after what had happened in the Mares' Hurdle the year before, was fantastic and seeing her gallop up the hill for victory was very, very special.

'Her performance in winning the Aintree Hurdle by 18 lengths was an amazing effort. Little did we think at that time that it would turn out to be her last race.'

'IT WAS GAS THE WAY IT TURNED OUT' – BRAVE INCA

It is Brave Inca that Colm Murphy (see page 162) will be especially remembered for.

The now prematurely retired trainer tells the story of his journey over to Cheltenham for the Supreme Novices' Hurdle with him; Tommy Woods was driving the lorry. It happened that the Lotto jackpot was €3 million.

'I asked Tommy if he would rather win the lotto than win the race at Cheltenham, and he said the Lotto. On the way home, after we had won, I asked him the same question, and he replied, "Cheltenham – you couldn't buy that."'

It was in 2001 that a group of nine friends decided to form a syndicate and try their hand at racing. One of them knew Colm's brother, and so they asked Colm to find them a horse. Their price limit was 10–12,000 punts. Colm went to the Goffs Land Rover sale for unbroken three-year-olds, and was under-bidder to several lots. It was nearing the end of the day, but he liked the look of a neat bright bay with a tiny white star, by Good Thyne out of the unraced Wigwam Mam, bred by Denis McCauley, who lives close to Downpatrick racecourse in Northern Ireland. It was the gelding's third visit to the sales, having been sold for 1,600 guineas as a foal, and £6,000 as a yearling. Now, aged three, the hammer fell to Colm Murphy's bid of 14,000 punts, enough over the budget limit to result in two proposed syndicate members deciding to withdraw.

It was left to Tony Crean and his two sons, Oran and Ronan, and Fergus O'Tierney and his three sons, Ciaran, Fionn and Boo, to form the Novices Syndicate. They chose the colours of purple jacket with yellow disc on body, and yellow sleeves and cap, which were to become so familiar to NH enthusiasts on both sides of the Irish Sea.

They also chose his name, Brave Inca. Seldom has a racehorse been better named, although it took a time for him to show his potential. Colm was only just getting going at the time and says, 'It was gas the way it turned out.'

A Supreme Novices' Hurdle, a Champion Hurdle, two Irish Champion Hurdles and ten Grade 1 wins from a total of fifteen could certainly be called 'some gas'.

It took Brave Inca a year to get into winning ways, after he was switched from moderate hurdle races to bumpers, with immediate effect, winning both his bumper races. Success breeds success, and Brave Inca re-embarked upon a hurdle career, winning five in a row, including at the top level. He beat future Queen Mother Champion Chase winner Newmill at Leopardstown before the 2004 Supreme Novices' Hurdle at Cheltenham. In this race, he beat future Gold Cup winner War Of Attrition by a hard-fought neck, showing his bravery for one of the regular good jockeys around, Barry Cash. The Irish went wild. They had sent the tenacious battler off as favourite.

Now they carried Colm Murphy on their shoulders in celebration. The partying continued for long hours, with members and friends of the Novices Syndicate spilling out of their tent onto a by-then-deserted concourse long after the last race had been run.

Brave Inca followed this by winning Ireland's Champion Novice Hurdle at Punchestown by an even closer margin of a short head from Royal Shakespeare.

In open company for the 2004–05 season, Brave Inca found life harder, winning once and placing second four times and third once. But what a third. In an epic Champion Hurdle, he was beaten a neck and a neck by Hardy Eustace and Harchibald. He then suffered an uncharacteristic fall in the Aintree Hurdle, the only time he fell in his illustrious career. Three weeks later, he won the Irish Champion Hurdle at Punchestown by a head from Harchibald.

Cheltenham beckoned again the next March, and following more successes in the run-up to it, he was sent off favourite for the 2006 Champion Hurdle. He had Irish eyes smiling again when, ridden by AP McCoy, he had a length to spare over long-time Irish rival Mac's Joy, trained by Jessie Harrington.

If the celebrations of 2004 had seemed great, they exceeded everything now, and Brave Inca came home to Wexford a hero.

2007 saw him finish runner-up in the Champion Hurdle, but leg trouble resulted in him missing the next season. After a healing break, and now reaching veteran status, he won the Leopardstown Champion Hurdle once more, but ran down the field at Cheltenham and Punchestown, before going into honourable retirement from racing – and into the new sphere of Racehorse to Riding Horse classes on the summer show circuit.

Always brave, Brave Inca epitomised all that is good about jump racing.

Barry Cash, who memorably rode Brave Inca in his first eleven hurdle races – and won the first five of them, including the 2004 Supreme Novices' – announced at Punchestown 2017 that he would be hanging up his racing boots. The forty-two-year-old had just shown all his skill in winning the four-mile one-furlong cross-country La Touche Cup on Treo Eile by a head over the odds-on favourite Cantlow.

NOT QUITE A CAPTAIN – FIRST LIEUTENANT

The term 'journeyman jockey' refers to a rider who is experienced, sound, and plies his trade well from day to day, without really hitting the heights.

A horse like First Lieutenant is often referred to as a 'good servant' in a stable. This is an equine equivalent to the journeyman jockey: consistent, always trying, often placing, occasionally winning, but all too often coming up against one or two better. Up until April 2017, First Lieutenant, trained by Mouse Morris, had run fifty times, forty-two of those in steeplechases. He had won three, was second nine times, and came third nine times. He ran twice in the Grand National, in which First Lieutenant most unusually fell at the second in 2016 – his first fall in his long and honourable career. Meanwhile, his stable companion Rule The World did just that by winning.

It was back in 2010 that First Lieutenant won a point-to-point on his debut, and swiftly followed that by winning a bumper; soon after, he won his first maiden hurdle. Winning the Grade 1 Future Champions Novices' Hurdle at Leopardstown that December by a neck at 16-1 encouraged connections to try for the 2011 Neptune Novices' Hurdle, run over two miles five furlongs at the Cheltenham Festival. Ridden by Davy Russell, it proved another thriller, with First Lieutenant beating future Champion hurdler Rock On Ruby by a short head. While that horse stayed hurdling,

First Lieutenant began chasing the following season. True to form, he won first time out, and he remained consistent. He was beaten in one novice chase by a nose, a new measure that was introduced in 2008 – even shorter than a short head, it equates to the width of a hair.

He was back at Cheltenham in 2012 for the RSA chase, in which he finished second of nine to future Gold Cup winner Bobs Worth.

The next season saw him consistently placing without quite winning, and it was the same for the 2013 Festival, when he was second to Cue Card in the Ryanair Chase. He followed this with a thoroughly deserved return to the winner's enclosure, winning the Betfred Bowl Chase at Aintree, beating Menorah.

This was his last win, but he kept on doing his best, and in 2017 he continued to place in easier races: a point-to-point, a hunter chase and a cross-country race. Unfortunately, he fell in the Festival's cross-country race. Now twelve years old, the Gigginstown-owned horse ran yet another gallant race to finish third in the four-mile one-furlong Cross Country Chase for the La Touche Cup in Punchestown, in late April 2017. After this, he was retired from racing, and will have a new life eventing for Eddie and Wendy O'Leary's daughter Megan. Chances are that Wendy may borrow him occasionally to hunt with the Westmeath Hunt, of which she is a joint-Master.

DIAMOND QUALITIES – FLORIDA PEARL

One of the first to put Willie Mullins on the map as a trainer was Florida Pearl. Consistent, reliable, almost always placed, he soon became a favourite with the crowds, blazing the way with his big white face. One of his most remarkable races was his last, in 2004, when he took the Irish scene to the greatest heights by winning his fourth Irish Hennessy after a gap of three years for owner Mrs Violet O'Leary. He also won the 2001 King George VI Chase at Kempton on Boxing Day, beating Best Mate.

Florida Pearl began his Cheltenham Festival record in great style, winning the 1997 Champion Bumper. Bypassing hurdling, he won the Royal & Sun Alliance Chase (now called the RSA) the following year. He looked all over a Gold Cup horse, and ran in NH racing's premier prize in 1999, when he was third to See More Business, and 2000, when he finished second to Looks Like Trouble. He missed the 2001 Festival, and in 2002 he was unplaced in the Gold Cup. 2003 saw him tried in the Queen Mother Champion Chase, but he was unplaced. His win at the Irish Hennessy at Leopardstown in February 2004 was one to bring tears to the eyes.

HARDY BY NAME, HARDY BY NATURE
– HARDY EUSTACE

Patrick Joyce, from near Thurles in County Tipperary, continued the family tradition of breeding when he bought the dam of Hardy Eustace, Sterna Star, for just £400 from friend and neighbour Philip De Vere Hunt, who had had a couple of foals out of her. When she had failed to breed for two years, he sold her to Patrick and his wife, Louise. From the family of the 1975 Arc winner Star Appeal, she only ran as a three-year-old, scoring once over one-and-a-half miles at Tralee.

This showed she had stamina, and so the Joyces chose to put her to Archway, who had been a smart sprinter for Vincent O'Brien, and was a half-brother to Derby winner Dr Devious. The stud fee was Ir 1250 guineas.

Eleven months later, the bay colt that was to be called Hardy Eustace was born. The Joyces put Sterna Star back to Archway, but she failed to conceive. She had three further foals by other sires, but then broke her hock and died. Such are the vagaries of breeding.

'Hardy Eustace was a beautiful foal,' says Louise Cooper-Joyce. 'He was majestic and extremely intelligent. He was also so laid back that he would remain lying down in his stable while the mucking out was done around him. He loved dogs and children, too.'

This continued while in training, as Dessie Hughes, who died in 2014, once told me: 'He's the kindest horse in the place. He eats, sleeps, and says "What do you want me to do?" and then tries to do it. I never have a day's worry with him, he's so laid back.'

He had joined Dessie Hughes' stable for Tullow, County Carlow, owner Laurence – Lar – Byrne. He named the bay after local land-owner Oliver Hardy Eustace-Duckett, born in 1899. Eustace-Duckett founded the Tullow Show, and was a member of the Irish National Hunt Steeplechase Committee.

The testing Cheltenham track brought out the best in Hardy Eustace. He won the 2003 Royal and SunAlliance Novices' Hurdle over two miles five furlongs, ridden by Kieran Kelly, who was tragically killed in Kilbeggan later that year. Hardy Eustace ran in the longer race, because he wasn't expected to have the speed for the Supreme Novices' Hurdle over the minimum two miles, let alone when older for the Champion Hurdle – which he promptly won in both the next two years. In the 2004 Champion Hurdle, it was the very knowledge that he stayed well that enabled his jockey, Conor O'Dwyer, to lead from flag-fall and test the stamina of his perhaps-swifter pursuers. His starting price of 33-1 in 2004 reflected what his chances were considered to be, but Hardy Eustace truly lived up to his name. When he was challenged at the last flight by the favourite and reigning Champion, Rooster Booster, he simply drew away up the hill to the winning post. This win put Dessie Hughes alongside Fred Rimell and Fred Winter, those select few to have both ridden and trained winners of the Champion Hurdle.

Lar Byrne had faith in his horse, and for his €240 placed on internet betting, he was reportedly rewarded with a payout of €62,000.

The punters made no mistake in the 2005 Champion Hurdle, sending him off joint-favourite with Edward O'Grady's Back In Front, who finished unplaced for jockey Ruby Walsh.

Hardy Eustace set off in front and ran the only way he knew, trying his hardest. He was challenged up the run-in by Harchibald and Brave Inca, but the tenacious Hardy held them off by a neck and a neck. Harchibald was given a trademark stalking ride by Paul Carberry, one of Ireland's most talented jockeys, who retired in 2016. He looked like winning, but when push came to shove, the horse declined to do so.

The breeder of Hardy Eustace, Louise Cooper-Joyce, still feels that he was underrated, even after his second win in the Champion Hurdle.

'Everyone just kept talking about Harchibald,' she says.

Hardy Eustace ran in the next two Champion Hurdles, coming third to Brave Inca in 2006 and fourth to Sublimity in 2007. In 2008, he was unplaced in the World Hurdle, and in 2009 unplaced back in the Champion Hurdle. His last win came in a two-mile hurdle race in Punchestown, in November 2008. The outsider of four, he showed all his old qualities to beat a certain horse called Sizing Europe – who was five years younger than him. Hardy even in old age, that was Hardy Eustace.

NOT TO BE SWATTED – HURRICANE FLY

Hurricane Fly. The Fly. One of the great Cheltenham winners, and a world record-breaker. Willie Mullins' face still lights up at the mention of his name.

'He was extraordinary,' he says simply.

Owned by Northern Irish business people and longstanding friends George Creighton and Rose Boyd, Hurricane Fly was bred at the Irish National Stud for Italian stud farm Agricola del Parc. He was sold for €65,000 at Goffs to go to France, where he won twice from ten starts on the flat, before being bought and returned to Ireland for Willie Mullins to train for hurdling. He quickly proved a revelation in this sphere, winning a twenty-five-runner maiden hurdle at Punchestown by twelve lengths on his first time out.

By the brilliant but sometimes fractious Montjeu, he progressed to become a dual winner of the Champion Hurdle, but it was in Ireland that he shone even brighter – in total, he won the world-wide record of twenty-two Grade 1 races. He was unbeaten at Leopardstown, winning all ten of his Grade 1 hurdles there, including five Irish Champion Hurdles.

But he proved vulnerable in Cheltenham. In spite of his Champion wins of 2011 and 2013, he was beaten into third place by Rock On Ruby in 2012. He was fourth to another Irish-trained horse, Jezki, in 2014. And in 2015, he was third to Faugheen, when Willie Mullins' horses filled the first three places; Arctic Fire was second.

Hurricane Fly possessed an aggressive determination to win, to be the best. He was always competitive, even at home – which meant he was not exactly the easiest horse to train or care for.

'You couldn't go into his stable without his permission,' Willie says in all seriousness. Anyone other than his lass, Willie's head girl Gail Carlisle, would have to give him a wide berth if they were walking along outside the stable or he would nip them.

Hurricane Fly was strong rather than big. He was still an 'entire' when purchased, and remained so for his first three or four races, prompting one to ask if connections were tempted to keep him as a colt, with a future as a stallion in mind (unusual for a NH horse). The idea was toyed with, but although gelded, he remained bold and coltish all his life – in terms of aggression rather than towards fillies. Even on the day his retirement was announced, in August 2015, Willie told the press that although he was rising twelve years old, he didn't know that, and was still a handful to ride.

He had a huge appetite – not just for food, but for life in general. He also travelled well, which helped on the journeys to Cheltenham.

Willie says, 'We hoped for a Cheltenham horse, but we never dreamed of twenty-two Grade Ones.'

What made Hurricane Fly so popular in Ireland was his small size, turn of foot and almost invariable wins. In total, he won twenty-four of his thirty-two hurdle races, was second three times, third three times and fourth once. The only time he was out of the frame was his last run, when he finished sixth in the 2015 French Champion Hurdle.

He also helped put Paul Townend on the map. Townend won his first Grade 1 on him, in the Royal Bond at Fairyhouse in 2008, when Ruby Walsh was sidelined because of a ruptured spleen. This was also Hurricane Fly's first Grade 1, and Paul was only seventeen years old. Paul rode him eight times and won six Grade Ones, with Ruby Walsh on board for all his other victories. Not surprisingly, Paul acknowledges him as playing a huge part in his career, paying tribute to Hurricane Fly's toughness and will to win.

In his early hurdling days, Hurricane Fly often came up against future World Hurdle winner Solwhit. He beat him four times, but Solwhit was to be victor once.

In later years, his big rival was Jezki, who won the 2014 Champion Hurdle. The Fly's stablemate, Thousand Stars, was also runner-up to him on three occasions.

Firey and always exciting to watch, Hurricane Fly in his early days was also capable of the occasional last flight blunder – that on every occasion he recovered to win only endeared him more to the Irish racing public.

As a four-year-old, he took on and beat his elders in the aptly-named Future Champion Novice Hurdle at Leopardstown by an impressive ten lengths. He was to be aimed for the Supreme Novices' Hurdle at the 2009 Cheltenham Festival, but injury ruled him out. He did not run again until November, when he was beaten by a neck by Solwhit. Another injury ruled him out of the 2010 Festival, when he would have contested the Champion Hurdle.

At last, in 2011, Hurricane Fly finally lined up at Cheltenham to land his first Champion Hurdle, in a hard-fought battle to the line against Peddlers Cross. The next year, Hurricane Fly suffered his only defeat in three seasons, Champion Hurdle victory going to Rock On Ruby. A year later, he turned the tables on his rival to regain the Champion Hurdle, a feat last achieved by the Fred Rimell-trained Comedy Of Errors back in 1975, having also won it in 1973.

For his fourth Irish Champion Hurdle, in January 2014, Hurricane Fly had had his preparation interrupted by a foot injury. He faced the brilliant but ill-fated Our Conor and future Champion Hurdler Jezki. Short of work he might have been, but even against such classy opponents, 'The Fly' put the race to bed with his scintillating speed from the last flight – racing into the record book with his nineteenth Grade 1 victory.

But a fourth place behind Jezki in Cheltenham, and a runner-up position to the same horse at the Irish National Hunt Festival at Punchestown in May 2015, made it look as if anno domini was catching up on the gutsy fellow.

Few would have been surprised to see him retired. Instead, he won his next three races, beating Jezki twice and finally Arctic Fire, Jezki having blundered at the last, for his fifth Irish Champion Hurdle. It was his last win, but he went down fighting to his younger stable companions, Faugheen and Arctic Fire, that March for the Champion Hurdle at the Cheltenham Festival. At eleven, he was the old man of the party, with his seven rivals being five, six and seven years old.

In what was to prove his penultimate race, he was tried over three miles for the first time, and was beaten into second by his old rival, Jezki. For his last run, in France over three-and-a-quarter miles, he could not get into contention and finished sixth.

Naturally, his two-mile speed had diminished, but the stayers distance did not seem to be for him. He came back into training after a summer break, and appeared as well as ever, but his owners made the sensible decision to call it a day.

By then he was eleven and, owing nothing to anybody, he went into honourable retirement, having amassed not much short of £2 million in prize money in his unforgettable career.

Owners George Creighton and Rose Boyd announced: 'He has produced us with so much joy for so long, and we're delighted to retire him at this time.

'Of course, a very big thanks must go to the family that is the Mullins yard, Harold Kirk (bloodstock agent), Gail (Carlisle), Paul (Townend) and Ruby (Walsh) to name a few. The door was always open to all our family members so they could be a part of this tremendous success story.'

Willie says of them, 'They realised and appreciated what they had, and really enjoyed him, and that others got fun out of him, too. They took his couple of setbacks well, and knew it was right, when he got a suspensory, to stop at once before making it worse.'

They were truly model owners.

Hurricane Fly now lives with other equine heroes Beef Or Salmon, Hardy Eustace, Kicking King and Rite Of Passage at the Irish National Stud in Tully, County Kildare. They can be seen and admired in their paddocks at the popular visitor centre there, which, along with the famed Japanese Gardens and Arkle Museum, is one of Ireland's top attractions.

For horse lovers and racing enthusiasts, it is a bonus to be able to see these living legends in honorable retirement.

SITTING TIGHT AND RIDING HIGH – MOSCOW FLYER

Jessica Harrington had some wonderful, and some heartbreaking, Festivals more than a decade ago with Moscow Flyer. In the Queen Mother Champion Chase, horses take fences faster than in any other steeplechase. In this event, a horse cannot afford to make a mistake, because at that speed it will almost inevitably lead to a fall or an unseat. This is what happened to Barry Geraghty in the year between his two Queen Mother successes on the popular horse, thus denying hopes of winning three years in a row.

In fact, during the main part of his career, Moscow Flyer won twenty races, interspersed with three unseats and two falls. This is how his form looked: 6343/1118/13121F21/F111F11/1U111/U111U1/111111/2245/

The son of Moscow Society was ridden by Barry Geraghty in all bar six of his forty-four races. He had to learn to sit tight; in 2003, the pair survived a mistake four out to beat another Irish contestant, Native Upmanship, trained by Arthur Moore, by seven lengths.

It was at the same fence in 2004 that Barry was catapulted onto the ground, leaving victory to Azertyuiop, but in 2005, and favourite for the third year running, the partnership remained intact. As usual, the remarkable horse was not foot-perfect at his bogey fence, but he beat Well Chief by two lengths.

Before his spinetingling Champion Chases, Moscow Flyer had also been a Grade 1 hurdler, and sparred with Istabraq a number of times. His final score was twenty-six wins from forty-four runs, including ten Grade Ones over fences and three over hurdles. He was retired after finishing unplaced in the 2006 Champion Chase, and was initially a star member of the Irish Horse Welfare Trust. Later, he was moved to the Irish National Stud, where he died in 2016 at the age of twenty-two from colic.

Jessie Harrington called him a 'horse of a lifetime'. Apart from his two Champion Chases, another of his most exciting wins came in the Tingle Creek Chase at Sandown in 2004.

Since the exciting days of Moscow Flyer, Jessie Harrington has steadily increased her stable at Moone, County Kildare, establishing her credentials as a top trainer. She has also branched out into flat racing with considerable success –shortly after the 2017 Gold Cup, she had three winners on the flat at Cork.

Jessie lost her much-loved husband Johnny in April 2014, just a month after she had won the Champion Hurdle with Jezki, ridden by Barry Geraghty. John Harrington was a highly respected bloodstock agent, and he had also originally held the training licence. He was a rock behind the business, and it is hugely to her credit that Jessie has continued in the form he would have believed in.

At Cheltenham in 2017, Jessie Harrington said, 'It's lovely to have winners here, because it's so hard. Every winner here is so special, and I remember every one of them. Space Trucker was the last festival race of the twentieth century when he won in '99. Then there's the great Moscow Flyer [three times], Spirit Leader in the County, Cork All Star in the bumper, Bostons Angel won the RSA and, of course, Jezki in the Champion Hurdle.'

Her three winners at the 2017 Festival, making eleven in all, make her the Festival's all-time leading woman trainer. They were Supasundae in the Coral Cup, Sizing John in the Gold Cup and Rock The World in the Grand Annual Chase.

SIX OF THE BEST – QUEVEGA

Willie Mullins has a soft spot for Quevega, and a note of surprise remains in his voice when he talks about her. For her to have won a second Mares' Hurdle at Cheltenham was a seemingly impossible feat in itself, but to do so an incredible *six* times in a row was, simply, a training feat of the highest class and an incredible act of faith.

Quevega was French-bred, by Robin Des Champs. She ran her first six races in France, winning the last three, before joining Willie Mullins' stable and finding new owners in the Hammer & Trowel Syndicate.

After her first Festival win in 2009, she suffered a hind leg injury. The vet, Ned Gowing, advised that she should go to stud. He felt it was touch-and-go whether she would recover sufficiently to make it back to the racecourse.

Willie says, 'I'm a great believer in horses for courses. I looked at her at home, and I thought she could possibly win a second time. The vet gave me a time-line for recovery, and I stuck to it, and got her there. Then it was whether she could do it again; it was a huge aspiration. I never dreamt it would or could be six times.'

Quevega had run once before in the season leading up to her first Festival win, in the new Mares' Hurdle in 2009. For her remaining five wins, she went straight to Cheltenham without any previous run, yet every time was fit enough to win. She also went on to win four World Series Hurdles at Punchestown in April. She ran her last race in 2014, and since then has given birth to a foal by Beat Hollow, a son of Sadler's Wells.

Willie gives a hint as to why some of his horses are seen so seldom outside of Cheltenham – he says that many others that do go by the wayside. Instead, he works from year to year, from Cheltenham to Cheltenham.

'They don't have to run anywhere else,' he says simply.

EUROPE'S FINEST HOUR – SIZING EUROPE

Waterford trainer Henry De Bromhead relates the story of Sizing Europe, a bright bay horse bred by Angela Bracken in County Offaly. Sizing Europe showed outstanding talent from the start. In January 2008, he beat former dual Champion Hurdle winner Hardy Eustace by an impressive eight lengths. This led to him starting as favourite for the 2008 Champion Hurdle. 'Europe' was such a poor traveller that Henry travelled in the trailer with him, soothing him frequently. But it seemed as if all his attention was in vain. At the important part of the race, Sizing Europe faded inexplicably to finish fourteenth of fifteen, leaving Henry De Bromhead 'absolutely gutted'.

While the connections of the winner, Katchit, celebrated, Sizing Europe was taken home. There, it was discovered he had damaged his sacroiliac joint, that place between the spine and pelvis that causes extreme pain when it 'goes'. Many months and much money were spent on therapy, and 'Europe' was able to race again the following season, 2008–09. Small problems held him up, however, and he only ran twice before the Champion Hurdle.

This time, poor Sizing Europe contracted transit fever in the ferry on the way over. This not only left him unable to run, but also meant he could not go home until he was well enough.

By May, he was well enough to run in the Punchestown Champion Hurdle, but his fourth place led the trainer to put him straight over fences later that month, with immediate success in a beginners' chase. Although this was in May, the NH season ends after the Punchestown Festival, and so this was officially in the new season, meaning he could remain in novice races in the autumn.

After his summer break, Sizing Europe took up where he had left off, beginning with the Buck House Novice Chase at Punchestown, where he jumped impeccably and beat Harchibald impressively. He added two more victories – at Punchestown and at the Leopardstown Christmas Festival, where he won a Grade 1 Novice Chase, beating Osana. In this, he had been challenged by Captain Cee Bee at the last fence, where that horse fell. There were many that day who considered Sizing Europe had been a lucky winner. Henry De Bromhead set out to prove otherwise, on behalf of owners Alan and Ann Potts.

After the failure in the 2008 Champion Hurdle, and his enforced non-appearance in 2009, Cheltenham and Sizing Europe were rapidly becoming a monkey on Henry's back.

Could it be third time lucky in 2010? Henry was openly hopeful about his chances in the Arkle Chase, for which he headed unbeaten over fences.

Captain Cee Bee was favourite, but broke a blood vessel. Sizing Europe pulled hard early on, and when leader Mad Max made a serious blunder two out, Sizing Europe, ridden as usual by Andrew Lynch, was left in the lead. He was chased by Somersby up the run-in, but held on by three-quarters of a length to record a first Festival win for both his trainer and jockey.

'People didn't know the problems he had had, and there are always people who are sceptical. It was fantastic,' says Henry. 'I was delighted as much for the horse as myself. He really proved himself that day.'

Henry spent that evening out with friends in a guest house on Cleeve Hill, before returning to his base at the Hunting Butts, the group of holiday cottages booked out by trainers, who enjoy its proximity to the course and their equine charges.

The step up from 'the Arkle' is usually 'the Queen Mother' or, on occasion, the 'big one', the Gold Cup, and that is where Henry set his sights for Sizing Europe in 2011. His build-up was not as impressive as before the Arkle the previous year. He travelled with Sizing Europe to Kempton that Christmas for the King George VI Chase on Boxing Day, an 'easier' three miles than Cheltenham. Snow and frost caused it to be postponed until two weeks later, but Henry decided not to make the return trip, as Europe was a notoriously bad traveller. Plans for the Gold Cup were put on hold, too.

Instead, Sizing Europe lined up for the 'Queen Mother' with two seconds and a third under his belt, with his regular rider, Andrew Lynch, in the saddle. The 2-1 favourite was dual winner Master Minded, ridden by Ruby Walsh for Paul Nicholls, with the previous year's winner, Big Zeb, at 3-1 and Somersby at 8-1. Sizing Europe's starting price was 10-1, with old adversary Captain Cee Bee on 14-1 and the remainder of the eleven runners at long odds.

'Europe' ran a blinder, and was four lengths clear of the favourite, Master Minded, when that horse blundered away his chance two out. Only Big Zeb could challenge the leader, getting to within half a length of Sizing Europe at the last fence, but this was to be 'Europe's' finest hour.

'Seeing him ping the last and leaving the others standing as he stormed up the hill was amazing,' Henry remembers. It is a memory that will remain with him forever.

It was a double celebration, too, as the previous day, Sizing Australia had won the cross-country race.

Speed inevitably gets blunted with age for two-mile horses, but Henry still hoped Europe might have enough stamina to become a Gold Cup prospect. He attempted three miles a few times but it was not to be, and instead the gallant horse ran in the Queen Mother Champion Chase for five consecutive years.

In 2012, he came in with two wins, including the Tingle Creek at Sandown, and a second, and was considered extremely unlucky not to win again. The last fence had been dolled-off and, in steering round it, Sizing Europe and challenger Finian's Rainbow bumped each other. Victory went to the Barry Geraghty/Nicky Henderson-ridden and trained Finian's Rainbow, with Big Zeb fifteen lengths back in third.

Sizing Europe ended his season by winning Ireland's Champion Chase at Punchestown, climaxing another successful season.

A year later, he was as good as ever, winning all three of his prep races for the 2013 Cheltenham Festival. He was now ten years old, yet he finished runner up again, to none other than Sprinter Sacre.

March 2014 saw his speed beginning to blunt, and he was fourth to Sire De Grugy in the Queen Mother, before regaining the Punchestown Champion Chase crown that he had lost to Sprinter Sacre the year before. He even won first time out in the autumn, taking the Grade 2 PWC Champion Chase at Gowran Park for the fourth consecutive year.

He was not so good next time out, but he still lined up for his fifth Queen Mother. It was the only time he was unplaced in this race, and afterwards he was honourably retired. Throughout his racing life, he was a model of consistency: in a total of forty-five racecourse appearances, he won or placed thirty-five times; his thirty-one steeplechases produced seventeen wins and ten places. His four unplaced attempts were all in older age, and two of those were fourths, which counts as 'in the frame'. The other two were his last runs, when age finally caught up.

He now takes pride of place in the Irish Horse Welfare Trust premises, set in the Wicklow Mountains and once the home of another famed 'Queen Mother' winner, Moscow Flyer. It is planned for him to take part in some of the Racehorse to Riding Horse classes that have become a feature of recent years, with pride of place being to compete at Dublin Horse Show. Sizing Europe had already attained a high standard in dressage whilst in training, so the chances must be that he will find himself winning in a different sphere before long.

Did you know that in this Champion Chase, there was a triple dead heat? It concerned the last three horses. Officially, Cornas finished a nose in front of Woolcombe Folly and Mad Max, who dead-heated, but with all three put down as finishing thirty-one-and-a-quarter lengths behind the winner, it made a most unusual triple dead heat.

MORE THAN A ONE-TRICK PONY – SUBLIMITY

The Artane area of Dublin's northside is probably better known for Beaumont Hospital or the Artane Industrial School than a Champion Hurdle winner.

The Ardlea Inn is owned by the Hennessy family. The main business of William Hennessy, who died in November 2016, was a hearing aid company in the city called Bonavox (good voice).

One day, a salesman called in to deliver hearing-aid batteries, and said, 'A friend of mine does a bit of busking, can he use your name?'

And thus was Bono born.

The shop still gets filled with souvenir hunters whenever Bono and U2 are playing in Dublin, and a knock-on effect is more business for the pub, too.

William Hennessy loved nothing more than his annual visits to the Cheltenham Festival. He had his first horse about thirty years ago, called On Offer – and he dreamed the dream. In due course, he began using a friend of his son Robert, trainer and dairy farmer John Carr in Maynooth, for pre-training, and then training.

Robert also rode out there regularly, and eventually William Hennessy decided he would like a 'Cheltenham' horse. He wanted a horse with more of a chance than those he had owned previously, and he set a budget of £50,000. He had hoped the year before to buy Essex, but was unsuccessful.

The horse had then won three races on the bounce – the Irish Cesarewitch on the Curragh, the Pierse Hurdle at Leopardstown and the totesport (formerly Schweppes) handicap hurdle at Newbury, before finishing unplaced in the 2005 Champion Hurdle. William Hennessy did not want to miss an opportunity like that again.

Robbie Hennessy accompanied John Carr to the Newmarket Sales, with a number of horses marked in the catalogue. One of these was a horse called Sublimity, with decent flat form. Trained by Sir Michael Stoute, he had won three races, including the listed Doncaster Mile Stakes, mostly running over one mile. As a yearling, he had cost 210,000 guineas at the Tattersalls October Sales.

By Selkirk, he looked a strong type that might adapt well to hurdling, but he came up quite late in the sale. They were about to leave empty-handed, but stayed to have a go for Sublimity.

When the hammer dropped to them for 32,000 guineas, they were at first delighted – but then the routine vetting afterwards showed up a possible flaw in his wind. The next morning, on Warren Hill, Newmarket, his wind came under further scrutiny before a panel of three vets.

By this time, and with the rumour mill working overtime, telling the young men that there was more than just his wind wrong with the horse, Robbie was praying the horse would fail the vet. He didn't, and Robbie Hennessy and John Carr were obliged to take him home, with William Hennessy having to pay up the purchase price.

Back at John Carr's base, the trainer set about schooling him over hurdles, with such good effect that they ran him in three schooling hurdles. These are held in Ireland, giving a young horse a chance to sample an atmosphere akin to racing and for trainers to assess their horse's ability before entering them for the real thing. They are held in Thurles and Fairyhouse, along with a few other courses.

Sublimity won all three, ridden by Philip Carberry, with no sign of any wind problems. Connections faced a pleasant dilemma. If they ran him in some hurdle races now, near the end of the season, he would lose his novice tag for the whole of next year. Instead, they entered him in the Group 3 Alleged Stakes on The Curragh, where, ridden by Johnny Murtagh, the pair made all and won – a nice bonus, especially as the prize to the winning owner of €32,550 as good as repaid Sublimity's purchase price.

Robbie Hennessy, previously a professional rider on the flat and then a conditional under NH rules, had been given pony-riding lessons in Malahide when he was about eight by his mother, Phyllis. At fifteen, he attended RACE, the Racing Academy and Centre of Education, based in Kildare. This is a school for jockeys, where pupils take school exams as well as having tuition in the art of race-riding, and the skill of looking after thoroughbreds. Robbie was placed with Dermot Weld for a year, and afterwards was apprenticed to Michael Kauntz near Ratoath, County Meath.

He was there for about four years, and placed a few times in rides on the flat, after which Michael Kauntz sent him to Australia to further his experience, where he rode three winners in Adelaide.

Once home, Robbie Hennessy was getting too heavy for the flat, and he began riding out for Tony Mullins, whose father, the legendary Paddy Mullins, trained a few horses for Robbie's father. At this time, Robbie was a claiming professional – that is, a conditional jockey claiming a weight allowance (akin to an apprentice on the flat) – and he rode about twenty NH winners in Ireland, mostly for his father.

One of his greatest experiences was to ride in the County Hurdle at the Cheltenham Festival in 1995, for Tony Mullins.

He recalls, 'I flew over the day before, and was very excited. I walked the course with Franny Woods, and he gave me tips. I was riding a horse called Kharasar.

'In the race, I had never been so fast in my life. It was a brilliant experience, even though I finished down the field [fifteenth of twenty-three]. I will never forget it; it was a one-and-only feeling.'

Racing for Robbie went on the back foot for a bit after that, and he worked in his father's pub for a few years, but he continued to ride out for Tony Mullins and John Carr.

He was still doing this at the time of Sublimity. The autumn of 2005 saw Sublimity entered for a maiden hurdle at Leopardstown, which he won easily by five lengths under Philip Carberry. It was immediately decided to send him for the Supreme Novices' Hurdle, the curtain-raiser at the 2006 Cheltenham Festival.

Philip Carberry rode a peach of a race at the Festival, but was helpless when a loose horse ran across their path on the sweep for home three out. In spite of being hampered so badly, Sublimity finished fourth, only three lengths behind the winner, Noland. Connections were disappointed, but justifiably thrilled at the prospect in their hands. They began to dream the dream – the 2007 Champion Hurdle, no less.

By this time, they had discovered that the prevalent heavy ground in Ireland was not for him. With his flat-race breeding, Sublimity was too delicate for it, and he didn't run often. He didn't run that autumn at all, with the ground too bad, and so for a pre-Cheltenham race he was sent to a lowly hurdle in Navan rather than one of the big Cheltenham trials elsewhere.

He duly won by twenty lengths, but this did not put him in the newspapers as a Champion Hurdle prospect; the correspondents were all talking about a rematch between Hardy Eustace and Brave Inca.

Robbie Hennessy thought otherwise, and told his pub regulars so. He was due to go to a local disco with Philip Carberry and other friends, but instead of going to the party, Robbie began backing Sublimity on Betfair. His first ante-post bets were at a massive 500-1. Robbie put on a number of bets of £25. The price reduced to 300-1, to 100-1 and then to 50-1; Robbie told his regulars to pile on. They did, in bets of £5 or £10, and soon the price was 25-1.

Robbie rode out on Sublimity every day, other than when his regular race pilot Philip Carberry came over. Philip had ridden a few winners for William Hennessy, and the ride remained his for the big stage.

By the time he started at Cheltenham, Sublimity was still one of the outsiders at 16-1. Five of the ten runners who lined up were trained in Ireland, but at the off the favourite was the Phillip Hobbs-trained Detroit City; Hardy Eustace was 3-1, and Brave Inca was on 11-2. Noel Meade had Iktitaf, and Tom Mullins was represented by the mare Asian Maze.

All the Hennessy family travelled over bar one of Robbie's brothers, Douglas, who stayed behind to look after the pub, helped by brother-in-law Anthony O'Rourke. The party consisted of William Hennessy, who booked rooms at the Chase Hotel in Gloucester Road, Cheltenham, sons Robbie and John, son-in-law Brian Kenny and various regulars from the pub. Robbie's mother Phyllis, who died two years later, stayed at home.

Robbie takes up the story of the race: 'We could see coming down the hill for the final time that Brave Inca and Hardy Eustace were hard at it up front, and Sublimity was travelling very sweetly behind them.

'Our boy was coming to challenge at the last, but made a hash of it and our hearts were in our mouths, but he drew away to win. We had to pinch ourselves.'

Brave Inca was three lengths behind, and Hardy Eustace was narrowly denied third by Afsoun, for Nicky Henderson and Mick Fitzgerald.

Of the inevitable party that followed, Robbie says, 'Lar Byrne stayed at the same hotel, and when he'd won the Champion Hurdle the year before with Hardy Eustace he put on a free bar, so my father did the same. The place was packed!'

The phone was hopping with journalists, and the party continued long into the night. Among them for the celebrations were Douglas Hennessy and Anthony O'Rourke, who, on seeing the race on television in their pub, had managed to book a flight over from Dublin to Birmingham. They hired a car and reached the Chase Hotel at five minutes to midnight, 'so they were able to say they were there on the day.'

Robbie thought back to the disco he had missed around Christmas time with Philip Carberry and friends. 'There had been a bit of drink taken, and in the morning, I didn't realise what I'd done. The drink had been talking – but I won between £30- and £40,000, so it was better than going to the disco!'

Robbie had always aimed long-term to train – he was too heavy to ride and did not want to be full-time in the pub. His father suggested that now was the time to start, while they had a good horse.

Sublimity stayed with John Carr for the following season, in which he finished fourth in the Champion Hurdle behind Katchit, and was second behind Punjabi in the Irish equivalent at Punchestown.

The following season Robbie rented a yard in Ratoath and took him on, along with about five other horses. Sublimity was his first runner, and travelled to Newcastle for the Fighting Fifth Hurdle, but it was postponed due to frost. Sublimity travelled back to Ireland and then, only a week later, headed back across the water to Wetherby, where the postponed race was to take place.

Sublimity ran a blinder, and was only just touched off by Punjabi by a head in the Grade 1 event. He went one better on home ground in the December Festival Hurdle at Leopardstown, where he beat Won In The Dark by half a length – Robbie Hennessy's first win, and it was a Grade 1 race.

All roads led to Cheltenham again, but the wind problems that had long promised finally rose to the surface, and he finished down the field. 'I was very disappointed, but Philip reported that he could hear his wind was not right,' remembers Robbie. The horse then had a soft-palate operation to help his wind.

Robbie and his wife Seana bought a small holding on the edge of Ratoath, with a neat house, a block of twelve stables and eleven acres of paddocks beyond. It has an aura of the typical, old-style small Irish trainer. He had an all-weather circuit laid down around it, and for longer gallops he boxes horses up to the Hill of Tara, near Skryne, or to Fairyhouse racecourse.

During his last three seasons, Sublimity ran with credit, placing almost every time he ran. Finally, in January 2011, he got his head in front again when, ridden by Andrew Lynch, he beat past Queen Mother Champion Chase-winner Newmill, in a hurdle race at Cork.

A new horse had come into Robbie's stable at this time – Rubi Light, which Philip Carberry had found in France. By winning the Grade 2 Red Mills Chase at Gowran Park, he earned a tilt at the Ryanair Chase, the feature on day three of the Cheltenham Festival. A blunder probably put paid to his chances, but his third place to Alberta's Run was a credit to him, to his jockey Andrew Lynch and his trainer Robbie Hennessy, who proved he was more than a one-trick pony.

'It was great to be back,' says Robbie, 'and he ran a cracker.'

The combination repeated the Red Mills win the following year, beating Chicago Grey. They again lined up for the Ryanair, and again ran well, without quite lasting up the finishing hill, to come seventh behind Riverside Theatre.

Cheltenham has become something of a home for such a small trainer, but sadly, in 2016, his father and principal owner, William Hennessy, died.

'It was like a wheel falling off,' says Robbie. In traditional Irish style, he can fall back on working in the pub, should he have to.

'I need new owners, but prices have gone crazy. To buy a horse like Sublimity at the Sales now would cost £200,000.'

He echoes the voices of many when he says that, but he remains optimistic.

MAKING THE GRADE – THOUSAND STARS

Another to touch the hearts of racing folk through his sheer consistency and toughness is Thousand Stars. Born in 2004, he ran some eighty times. Stalwart is a word that springs to mind for this evergreen grey, chiefly trained by Willie Mullins and owned by the Hammer & Trowel Syndicate, comprised of bricklayer Sean Deane and carpenter Ger O'Brien, who formed the partnership at a Christmas party. Apart from Thousand Stars and superstar Quevega, they also owned J'y Vole, another successful mare. The greatest memory for many of Thousand Stars is when he won the 2010 Vincent O'Brien County Hurdle at the Festival, ridden by Katie Walsh at odds of 20-1. First to congratulate her was her brother, Ruby, on the Paul Nicholls-trained favourite, who had been badly hampered and finished twenty-third.

Before he came to Ireland, Thousand Stars ran no less than twenty times as a two- and three-year-old in his native France, winning twice. He was to return to France, to Auteuil, many times during his illustrious career. It took a while for him to get off the mark in Ireland, finally winning a maiden hurdle in Killarney in 2008. But, after his County Hurdle victory two years later, he was stepped up to graded races, and ran in both the Champion Hurdle of 2011 and the World Hurdle a year later. He often came up against the stable star Hurricane Fly, but he won four Grade Ones, and was frequently placed in Grade 1 races.

Auteuil became a stamping ground for him. He twice won the Grande Course d'Haies d'Auteuil, the French Champion Hurdle, under Ruby Walsh – in June of 2011 and 2012. In May 2014, Katie Walsh rode him to victory there in the Grade 2 Prix La Barka, traditionally the warm-up race for the French Champion.

His last run at the Cheltenham Festival was in the 2012 World Hurdle, when he was fourth to Big Bucks.

When horses like Thousand Stars come up against their era's star horse, it can be hard to find the right races for them, and for the grey the answer to avoiding Hurricane Fly lay in France. He will be fondly remembered.

INTO BATTLE – WAR OF ATTRITION

War of Attrition was one of Michael O'Leary's early horses, an attractive bay by Presenting, bred by Miss BA Murphy. He fell at the last fence in a point-to-point that he 'would have won by a minute', according to Eddie O'Leary. The horse that finished fourth that day won next time by a fence, and the fifth-placed horse won by twenty lengths the following week. It was clear that War of Attrition was high-class, and he was turned away for summer grass after that introduction, that vital holiday turned out in lush pastures, also known as 'doctor green'.

War of Attrition was one of the first young O'Leary horses to come to Dot Love, outside Mullingar, for pre-training. She remembers he was 'always a very good mover, with the right attitude, and jumped well. Mouse Morris (who trained him) always thought highly of him, too.'

As a novice hurdler, he was beaten by a neck by Brave Inca in the Supreme Novices' Hurdle at Cheltenham, and as a novice chaser, he suffered a fractured hind splint bone at Thurles that kept him box-bound for eight weeks. This meant he contested the 'Arkle' with the experience of only two steeplechases, both of which he had won. But his seventh in the Arkle probably did not put him in too many people's books as the next year's Gold Cup winner.

He ended the season by winning at Punchestown, and began the next in similar style, beating the reigning Gold Cup holder, Kicking King, in October, and Rathgar Beau in November. These wins could have been seen as a signal of the future, but he was then beaten by both Hi Cloy and Beef Or Salmon prior to Cheltenham.

Racing quickly became Michael O'Leary's way of relaxing, but the Ryanair boss never quite takes his eye off the ball. That year, 2006, he ensured that there would be a flight desk at the track for his newly-sponsored Ryanair Chase on the Thursday of Cheltenham. For a long time this race seemed the obvious target for War of Attrition – what better publicity for the boss, after all. But he left it to the trainer, and was rewarded with the ultimate jumping prize.

The horse was beautifully ridden by Conor O'Dwyer. He gave the comparative novice plenty of room to see his fences and this fine young horse was literally spring-heeled over the last two fences, putting paid to the tenacious challenge of Aintree hero Hedgehunter.

'I think I've died and gone to heaven,' an understandably delighted Michael O'Leary said afterwards. 'I never thought it would happen; it's unbelievable.'

A month later, War Of Attrition franked that form by beating Beef Or Salmon in the Guinness Gold Cup at Punchestown.

In his career, War Of Attrition won or placed in twenty of his twenty-four chases. He retired to the Westmeath hunting field in the hands of Cian Murphy, taking the many and varied obstacles, and the sometimes 'bottomless' ground, like an old hand. As I write, he is living out his days on Michael O'Leary's Gigginstown Stud.

The old Irish currency featured a variety of animals on one side of the coins, and the one on a half-crown (two shillings and sixpence) was of a rather fine-looking horse. A friend of mine from County Galway, the late Tom Walshe, told me of a couple of guys who took a stash of them to Cheltenham, and sold them as being of Arkle, for five guineas each. When someone asked what the '2s 6d' stood for, quick as a flash up came the answer, 'It's Irish for miles and furlongs.'

CHAPTER 5

COGS IN THE WHEEL – INTEGRAL PLAYERS

BREEDER/BLOODSTOCK AGENT – LUCKY LOUISE

To have sourced two Gold Cup winners – Mr Mulligan and Looks Like Trouble – and bred a dual Champion Hurdle winner – Hardy Eustace – is the admirable record of Tipperary's Louise Cooper-Joyce. A second cousin to young star jockey Bryan Cooper, through Bryan's grandfather and Louise's father being brothers, Louise grew up with Cheltenham in her blood. Her father, Brian, who was first jockey to Barney Nugent, rode many times at the Cheltenham Festival during the 1940s and 1950s, and Louise has been a regular since she was eleven or twelve years old. One of the first horses she remembers was a mare called New Year's Eve, who won many races, but then failed to breed.

As soon as the Irish rules allowed it, Louise began NH race riding herself. She was the first woman to ride in Punchestown, and she won the 1975 Ladies Cup over banks on a horse called New Road, trained by Danny Keating. She had won a point-to-point on him, but had no licence to ride under NH Rules. Following a visit by her parents to a couple of stewards the night before, she was handed her licence at the scales. She had walked the course with Jack Hartigan, of the Kildare Hunt, and Eddy Harty's head lad Frank McCormack. They advised her not to jump the famous Big Double (of banks) on the inside, where it was higher, but to go for the middle. She beat John Fowler, who was second, and third-placed Ted Walsh.

'There was no trophy presentation in those days,' she recalls. 'We just had to go to the secretary's office to collect the cup.'

She was also the first woman to ride a winner in Navan, on a mare called Highway Peak, trained by her father. 'It was a bumper run in a dreadful snow storm, I'll never forget it!'

In time, Louise began buying and selling as well as breeding. One of her long-standing patrons is Michael Worcester, for whom she found Mr Mulligan and Looks Like Trouble.

Another Gold Cup connection for Louise came when she bought the dam of 2015 Gold Cup winner Coneygree, Plaid Maid, for £5,000 from Mick O'Toole for the Bradstock family. Sarah Bradstock's father, the inimitable and much-missed amateur rider and writer par excellence Lord Oaksey, had agreed to set up a syndicate. The budget was £2–3,000; Louise managed to persuade them that this was not enough, and the purchase of Plaid Maid resulted.

'She was not big,' remembers Louise, 'but she was well built.'

Plaid Maid did not race, but produced five foals, unfortunately dying while giving birth to the last one. There has long been a feeling in racing that first foals may be inferior, but Plaid Maid's first foal was as game as they come, the much-loved Carruthers, whose ten wins from forty-three runs included the 2011 Hennessy Gold Cup. Lord Oaksey was aging at this time, and the horse was a great tonic. Waiting in the wings was Coneygree, the first of whose wins came shortly before Lord Oaksey died in 2012.

Louise and her husband Patrick Joyce have long been involved in breeding. In fact, Patrick's father Martin bred a number of NH horses, amongst whom was the good chaser Duke of Milan. His brother Tommy and brother-in-law Paddy Finn bred the 1963 Champion Hurdle winner Winning Fair, ridden by competent amateur Alan Lillingston.

Patrick and Louise will be especially remembered for breeding Hardy Eustace, whose story is told on page 101. They also bred His Song, by Accordian; he was sold into the ownership of tennis star David Lloyd, and won four hurdles and five chases when trained by Mouse Morris. He was also second in the 1998 Supreme Novices' Hurdle at the Festival, and in subsequent years also ran in the 'Arkle' and the Cathcart Chase, without placing.

Louise keeps busy with her bloodstock agency, while at home they have reduced their number of mares on their 200 acres near Thurles, instead taking in mostly flat boarders for foaling and bringing on.

OWNERS

One of the enduring charms of horse-racing is its diversity, not least in some of its owners. These include the super-rich, and in Ireland that means people like Ryanair supremo Michael O'Leary. O'Leary, with his brother

Eddie, has more than seventy horses with Gordon Elliott alone, and many more with several other trainers around Ireland, under their Giggingstown House Stud banner.

JP McManus also has numerous horses spread around many trainers, large and small, on both sides of the Irish Sea. These include about thirty-five with Jonjo O'Neill at Stow-on-the-Wold. Rich Ricci, the English-based American, keeps his and his wife's horses with Willie Mullins in County Carlow because, he is reported in the *Racing Post* as saying, 'I just love Irish racing. The people are fantastic, the atmosphere is really good and the prize money is still attractive. My wife [Susannah] and I get a real buzz from it.'

By contrast, there are many owners of single, or only a few, horses, and many syndicates. Syndicates and other forms of multiple ownership have proved the way for people of modest means to get into and enjoy racehorse ownership. I shall never forget seeing the joyous celebrations of the Novices Syndicate, owners of the heroic Brave Inca, on his first visit to the Festival.

Back in the day, Irish racing was the poor relation to its bigger neighbour across the water, and every time Ireland produced a promising and well-bred horse, which was frequent, it was almost inevitably sold to England. Apart from a handful of exceptions, when a horse was sold, that was it, it was gone, because Ireland in those days was very poor.

Things gradually improved, and prior to the financial crash of 2008, many new owners had been recruited in Ireland, and racing was in a healthy condition. Many of the new owners were property developers or the recipients of the proceeds of land sold for building. There were many enthusiastic syndicates, and, of course, there was JP McManus.

Michael O'Leary entered racehorse ownership in a quiet way, with just two horses, early in the new Millennium. Today he is a mammoth owner, and his presence is both successful and, at times, vocal.

The merry-go-round of some big owners with trainers in Ireland illustrates how tenuous a relationship can be, no matter how many big-race victories may have been achieved on their behalf. Others put loyalty and/or the joy of having horses with someone they regard as a friend first.

'A GREAT ORANGE THING'
– ALWAYS DREAMING OF CHELTENHAM

Michael Worcester, based near Bristol, was a keen hunting man with the Berkeley Hunt, and his first foray to Ireland was ostensibly to buy a hunter. He returned with a thoroughbred called Midnight Caller, who went on to win seven races, trained by Simon Sherwood. In the first of these, Michael Worcester placed £40 on him ante-post at 40-1.

'There were twenty-three runners, and he hacked up.'

His next horse, Mr Mulligan, found for him by Louise Cooper-Joyce, was a big, white-faced chestnut by Torus, which he described as 'a great orange thing'. He was certainly no oil painting, and he had already failed the veterinary inspection for three previous would-be owners due to a heart murmur when Michael Worcester bought him.

'I took a chance on it,' he remembers, 'and, as it happened, his heart was one thing that never went wrong for him.'

Mr Mulligan did not, however, make an auspicious start, with Fell, Slipped Up and Brought Down being his first point-to-point results, followed by a win.

Michael Worcester decided to set up a private trainer. He chose Dublin-born, Downpatrick-educated Noel Chance, who at the time was training on The Curragh, and installed him in Lambourn, with magic results.

Once sold to England, Mr Mulligan again fell in his first chase, but thereafter, for Noel Chance, he won an impressive five novice chases in a row, by wide margins. Now he was Cheltenham bound. He came up against one too good in Nathan Lad in the 1996 Sun Alliance Chase. Next season, 1996–97, an initial fourth and a fall in the King George at Kempton did not augur well, but nevertheless he lined up for the Cheltenham Gold Cup at odds of 20-1, ridden by Tony McCoy. He took a clear lead in the latter stages, and beat the consistent Barton Bank easily.

Mr Mulligan only had two more career runs, due to a tendon injury. In these two races, he finished second and then bowed out with a win. Later, he was kicked in the field by Michael Worcester's hunter, broke a leg and had to be put down.

On the day of Mr Mulligan's Gold Cup victory, Michael Worcester had the money in his pocket to pay Louise Cooper-Joyce for Looks Like Trouble, her next Gold Cup find.

'We met by the Arkle statue, but not until after Mr Mulligan won,' she recalls.

A slow developer, Looks Like Trouble finally reached the winner's enclosure in January 1999 on his eighth attempt, at 20-1, ridden at Doncaster by Irishman and now TV racing presenter Mick Fitzgerald. By this time, and because he 'needed some money', Michael Worcester had sold him on.

The horse remained in Noel Chance's yard, and swiftly made it a hat-trick, at Sandown after Doncaster and then winning the Royal Sun &

Alliance Chase at the Cheltenham Festival, ridden by fellow Irishman Paul Carberry. A year later, 2000, with two more wins under his belt, he lined up for the Cheltenham Gold Cup, and was ridden to victory by Richard Johnson over Irish-trained Florida Pearl (one of Willie Mullins' first runners in the race).

More recently, Louise has been able to help Michael Worcester again. After his initial foray into ownership, he gave up for a while, but more recently decided he would like to have something to run in Ireland. Louise was able to put him in the way of another deserved trainer starting out, former top amateur Robbie McNamara. Michael Worcester was happy to take Louise's advice, but she urged him to come over and meet the rookie trainer. Michael Worcester had forgotten at the time that the former top amateur had been paralysed in a fall at Wexford, but after dinner in Chez Hans in Cashel, a deal was done between the three of them.

Robbie's injury had happened just thirteen months after his greatest riding feat, when he scored a double at the 2014 Cheltenham Festival. He won the Champion bumper for flat maestro trainer Dermot Weld on Dr Ronan Lambe's Silver Concorde, and the Fulke Walwyn Kim Muir Amateur Riders' Chase on Spring Heeled, trained by Jim Culloty.

Support for Robbie as he embarked on training from a wheelchair was widely forthcoming. Such was his own determination that, just fifteen months after the fall, in July 2016, he trained a double with his first two runners, at the Cork summer meeting.

The first was Chadic in the maiden hurdle for Dr Ronan Lambe, for whom he had won Cheltenham's Champion bumper, and he followed that up with the concluding bumper with Rathcannon for Michael Worcester.

Since then, Louise has sourced another from Jim Culloty for Michael Worcester in Quick Grabim and, after an initial half-length second in a Cork bumper, connections were approached by representatives of Gigginstown House Stud to see if he might be sold. The answer was no. Quick Grabim next recorded an impressive win in a Leopardstown bumper at Christmas, after which a JP McManus representative knocked on their door, figuratively speaking. The answer was again no, and Quick Grabim became Robbie McNamara's first Festival runner in 2017, but he finished unplaced in the Champion Bumper.

Michael Worcester has just four horses in training – in addition to Rathcannon and Quick Grabim, he has Cosmo's Moon and an as-yet-unnamed youngster by Konig Shuffle. Michael does not pay big money for his horses, and smiles when he remembers some he's been offered: there was one he was offered for €150,000 – 'not my cup of tea' – and another for €250,000.

Instead, he has bought the Konig Shuffle youngster for €12,000.

'He is my dark horse,' he says. 'He is a beautiful chestnut individual, and the signs are that all four horses are up to Cheltenham standard. I'm always dreaming of Cheltenham.'

THE PATRON SAINT OF NATIONAL HUNT RACING – JP MCMANUS

If you saw 'JP' walking down the street of a small Irish town, you would think he was an off-duty parish priest – smiling, acknowledging people, accessible. John 'JP' McManus, one-time JCB driver, bookmaker and finally hugely successful punter and financier, is not only known as a racehorse owner, but also for his philanthropy. Unknown is just how much he actually gives for good causes, be it somebody in racing down on their luck, or a local GAA club, or a worthy charity. It is known that his 'minders' may be approached to ask for support, and if JP agrees, he is likely to add that he does not want it spoken about.

JP's familiar green-and-gold striped colours, representing the South Liberties GAA Club in Limerick, are worn by the many horses that he owns, spread widely around different trainers, in addition to those trained at his Jackdaws Castle yard in the Cotswolds by his incumbent, Jonjo O'Neill (see page 175). Loyalty is a key part of JP as an owner, and he has been life's blood to many a small trainer. This is because when he, or his racing manager Frank Berry, sees a promising horse that he would like to buy, after purchase he invariably leaves it with the current trainer, often giving them a leg up in the process.

JP loves his horses, and for decades he has practised a policy of retiring them to his farm in Martinstown, County Tipperary. There they are pampered for the rest of their lives.

His first racehorse, Cill Dara, won the Irish Cesarewitch, but most of JP's interest as an owner is in jumping. He loves the pleasure a good horse gives, but from the start he recognised that both the trainer, and the horse's lad or lass, derive equal pleasure. This is partly why he has the admirable policy of not moving a horse from its current yard after he buys it.

His first Cheltenham Festival winner was Mr Donovan, in the two-mile five-furlong Novices' Hurdle in 1982, trained by Edward O'Grady and ridden by Tommy Ryan. The race has been named after various sponsors, Royal Sun Alliance/RSA, Ballymore Properties, and currently Neptune. Its registered title is Baring Bingham, after the founder of the Cheltenham Festival in 1902.

In 1978, JP looked like achieving his first Cheltenham win with Jack of Trumps in the four-mile NH Chase, but lost his jockey. He has been quoted as saying that, had he not had that win with Mr Donovan four years later, he might have quit trying. It is just as well that he got that win, because a few more lean years followed, with only one or two winners in the 1990s, until the advent of Istabraq.

The first of Istabraq's three wins was especially emotional, because the person who found, and believed in, Istabraq – John Durkan – had just died, at the age of thirty-one. It was a game-changer – and charged with emotion.

In later years, and with both Istabraq and Charlie Swan retired, the era of AP McCoy began, with Binocular winning the 2010 Champion Hurdle; Synchronised the 2012 Gold Cup; and a good many more. Once AP retired, his place was taken as retained jockey by Barry Geraghty, who has only Ruby Walsh ahead of him in terms of most wins at the Cheltenham Festival.

A week-and-a-half before the 2017 Cheltenham Festival, JP's promising juvenile Charlie Parcs was odds-on to win at Kempton Park, but was already being niggled along when he failed to answer jockey Barry Geraghty's call for a good jump at the penultimate flight. The pair took a crashing fall, but, while the horse got up okay, Barry received a nasty kick.

Only a short while later, the television cameras showed him being loaded into the ambulance, and there to see him off, with a little wave, was JP himself.

'He is the Patron Saint of National Hunt racing,' says Charles Powell, a Tipperary man. 'JP loves horses, the countryside, the people. His generosity to the community is colossal, much of it unknown; he doesn't do it for social aggrandisement.'

That sums up the man.

At Cheltenham in 2017, JP had a massive total of 119 entries; from those declared, he had three winners. Buvair D'Air not only won him his sixth Champion Hurdle (a record), but also topped his half-century of Festival winners, a total far in excess of any other owner at Cheltenham, either currently or in the past.

> For Cheltenham taxi driver Andrew Brookings, the Festival is naturally a busy time. One year, he had two Irish footballers in the back of his cab; he took them to the top-end luxury Ellenborough Hotel, where Niall Quinn and JP McManus came up to greet them.
>
> 'There was a big celebration going on,' he remembers. 'The Irish are super, I've been ferrying them for very many years.'

O'LEARY'S FLYING HORSES – GIGGINSTOWN HOUSE STUD

Michael O'Leary began with two horses. One of them, Tuco, was bought at the Land Rover sales, with a view to winning the Land Rover bumper. This he duly did, first time out, beating twenty-six others. Tuco won three of his first five runs, prompting his trainer, David Wachman, to predict he would be best over fences.

'We'll look after him, and won't take on the best novice hurdlers,' he told the press. But even the best-laid plans can go awry and, sadly, Tuco fell in a hurdle race and broke a leg at Fairyhouse soon after.

At one stroke, Michael O'Leary, who had chosen the Westmeath colours of maroon-and-white to represent his home county, had lost fifty percent of his stable. He was gutted. But he was not afraid to invest in more horses.

One of the new horses was Night Busker, who climaxed his five wins from eleven runs for trainer Dessie Hughes by taking the Midlands National in Kilbeggan, on only his third run in a steeplechase. This is the local course for Michael O'Leary, and he was on hand to receive the trophy and to talk to the late, much-missed broadcaster Colm Murray in the paddock afterwards.

Michael O'Leary is inclined to set the sky as the limit, as anyone with Ryanair experience knows (and that probably includes most people in Ireland). He does nothing by half measures, and once he makes a commitment, he sticks to it. He has seen the downside of NH racing, and also the ultimate: to date in 2017, two Gold Cups, with War Of Attrition and Don Cossack, and a Grand National with Rule The World.

Away from the office, he likes nothing more than to see his black Aberdeen Angus cattle, and retired and young racehorses, on his Gigginstown House Stud, nestling in attractive countryside and narrow lanes off the main road between Mullingar and Delvin.

Michael O'Leary is the first to admit that there are other key players in his now racing empire. It is led by his brother Eddie, of Lynn Stud in Killucan, Westmeath, who masterminds much of the enterprise and finds the horses.

Many of the young purchases are broken and pre-trained by Dot Love of Charlestown Stud, Mullingar, and her right-hand man, Ciaran Murphy. Dot Love memorably won the 2013 Irish National with Liberty Counsel at 50-1. The horses are spread out among a number of trainers throughout most of Ireland, chiefly Gordon Elliott.

'All I do is sign the cheques,' Michael O'Leary is apt to quip.

KEEPING THE SHOW ON THE ROAD
– RACING SECRETARIES

Zoe Winston, racing secretary to Gordon Elliott, has been with him since he was a small, unknown trainer in Capranny, outside Trim in County Meath. His one broken-down horse, bought for some cross-country races, had just happened to win the Grand National at Aintree before Gordon had yet had a single winner in Ireland.

It means that she understands his every move, and probably every thought, despite the stable having grown into almost certainly Ireland's largest. Its capacity is 200, and it is often full.

The daughter of top Yorkshire-based Irish trainer Ferdy Murphy, Zoe is married to John Winston (brother of flat jockey Robert Winston), and they live in the original house at Cullentra, Longwood, County Meath.

She is happy to take a visitor round for a tour of the horses and the expanding facilities, and, like Nicole Kent at Henry de Bromhead's, she works out of a portacabin. It is a matter of the horses' comforts coming first.

Zoe had been at Gordon's for three years when she decided she wanted a career change, and went off to work in the Brown Thomas department store in Dublin.

'I was very wrong,' she readily admits.

Her young working life was spent with her father for ten years, including as assistant trainer and training a few point-to-pointers. She spent a few months in Spain, and has ridden out for many trainers, but since having her son, Tighe, six years ago, she has given that up. She is due another baby in October 2017.

When Gordon Elliott was looking for a part-time secretary for two days' work a week, she jumped at the chance; after only three months, it became a full-time position. The work includes doing 'anything and everything', from the entries and declarations, to talking to owners and checking horse passports, to helping some of the work riders obtain licences to race. All of them will be given opportunities – if they work hard and are ready for it. She is responsible for booking Gordon's frequent flights, and in addition she runs the Gordon Elliott Racing Club, along with web designer Dean Walker.

The club is a marvellous way for anyone with even the slightest interest in racing, and even the smallest of purses, to get involved, and has about 150 members at present.

'They're a great bunch of people,' Zoe says. She sends them daily emails with updates about their four horses, which have scored four wins. As the club membership increases in size, so will its number of horses.

Another task for Zoe is responding to the increasing number of invitations to Gordon. He goes to the majority, and only declines those that he simply can't get to.

Zoe adds that all owners receive the same treatment, from the one-horse syndicate to the big player.

It's a busy office – and Zoe is definitely looking forward to the purpose-built one.

'The portacabin is freezing in winter,' she says. 'And a new one will give me more storage so that I can have everything organised and put away properly.'

* * *

Nicole Kent has been with Henry de Bromhead as secretary and rider since 2014. She originally worked for Market Rasen racecourse in her home county of Lincolnshire, and then came to work for Charlie Swan in Tipperary 'for a couple of months'. That has turned into seventeen years. Nicole is married to Henry De Bromhead's head lad/assistant Davy Roche, and she is the mother of Harry, aged nine.

Her enthusiasm for all of Henry's charges is infectious. It's his best ever season, and although he lost thirty or more of Potts-owned horses, he gained a number belonging to Gigginstown House Stud, aka Michael and Eddie O'Leary after their split with Willie Mullins, adding to those they already had with him.

Nicole's job is typical of many racing secretaries, who ride out in the morning and then work in the office. The office in Nicole's case is a small portacabin close up to a wall in the original old farmyard. It doubles up as racing room, storing owners' colours, and is a meeting point for visitors and copious cups of tea. Henry wanders in, phone clapped to his ear, goes through a few declarations and entries with Nicole and then leaves her to it.

Nicole says, 'My job is riding out a couple in the morning, before coming in to do the decs and entries. I deal with the owners and do all the paperwork for their horses. I do the accounts, the banking, paying of bills, etc.'

Nicole recalls accompanying Special Tiara to Kempton in 2016, travelling in a jeep and trailer. She was able to spend Christmas Day with her family not far away. On Boxing Day, her husband, Davy Roche, rode 'Mr T' out in the centre of the course for an early-morning pipe opener.

Growing up a fan of Richard Dunwoody, Nicole was thrilled to meet the retired jockey there. He comes every Boxing Day to pat the bronze statue of Desert Orchid, on whom he won the last two of 'Dessie's' four King George VI Chases.

It is also a great day for Special Tiara, who, having missed the race in 2015, won his second Desert Orchid Chase in the hands of Noel Fehily on December 27 2016.

Little did Nicole guess what was to come three months later for Special Tiara when, at his fourth attempt, he won the 2017 Queen Mother Champion Chase (see page 219), for his sporting American owner, Mrs Sally Rowley-Williams.

Nicole had been left behind to hold the fort. She says, 'I watched the Champion Chase at home with Harry. We were both screaming at the telly, it was unreal; I knew he'd win jumping the last, he was just amazing …!!!

'We didn't celebrate at all, as Henry was in Chelt, and we had the yard to keep going here!'

STABLE LADS AND LASSES

Girls love horses. Nowhere is this more evident than in horse-racing, and it's true of many of the lads, too. They look after their charges day in, day out, picking up poo, minding the occasional horse who kicks or bites, cleaning their 'tickly' bits.

Anyone can enjoy riding across the countryside on a beautiful sunny morning on a sleek thoroughbred, but these lads and lasses do it in all weathers – on bitterly cold mornings, or with the rain pelting down. Generally, they manage to do so with plenty of banter among themselves.

On race day, they will be polishing and plaiting 'their' horse; they will be tending to his every need, patting his neck and whispering encouragement, especially if the horse is suffering from pre-race nerves, or if the excitement of the occasion is getting the better of him.

Then it is standing at his head, a hand each side of the reins, while he is saddled up, and leading him out to parade round the paddock. Once the jockey is mounted, she or he leads them out to the racetrack and lets off the lead rein. Now, both trainer and groom have done their bit; the jockey is solely in charge of the horse. The lad or lass may watch from an area designated for them, or look at the big screen or, perhaps, disappear out of sight, into hiding, too afraid to watch the horse they know inside out, who they care for and love – that is not too strong a word.

A nice trend today is that the groom, male or female, is acknowledged by the TV coverage, and sometimes briefly interviewed. In another innovation to be applauded, at places like the Cheltenham Festival they are brought up to the winner's rostrum to be given a prize or memento alongside the winning owner, trainer and jockey – that is, if they are not off hosing their horse down, and making him comfortable. All the other grooms of the unplaced horses will already be doing this, unsung, just getting on with their jobs. The worst is when their horse doesn't come home at all.

Some lads or lasses become well known because luck has given them a horse that becomes famous. Two that spring to mind are Johnny Lumley, who was Arkle's lad in the 1960s – his picture was frequently in the papers holding the great horse – and, in more recent times, Willie Mullins' head girl Gail Carlisle, who was often photographed with Hurricane Fly. Sometimes articles were written about her and her role, as well as about the horse.

It is a good long while ago that prizes crept in for the groom of the horse adjudged to be Best Turned Out, and they are now universal, including for point-to-points. Again, it is a means of acknowledging the work that goes on by lads and lasses behind the scenes.

CHAPTER 6

ALWAYS LOOKING FOR A CHELTENHAM HORSE – TRAINERS

WHEN IRISH EYES ARE SMILING – WILLIE MULLINS

It was the four-mile amateur riders' race, and the mare, a faller in her last race at Fairyhouse, had been popping away, until she took over the lead. One or two horses were near her as she swept round the final bend, her rider's head down briefly as he urged his mount to extend her advantage approaching the last fence. The last fence. It wasn't there! For one awful, mind-blowing moment, the amateur thought he must have taken the wrong course. Was his Cheltenham dream of a first win on a first ride here about to be shattered? It only took a blink of an eye, and when he looked again, the fence was there all right – it may have been masked by a shadow for a fraction of a second. The pair soared over and galloped on to victory.

William Patrick Mullins didn't let on widely about his momentary scare. Instead, he savoured the reception, especially that of Indian-born, Dublin-reared Roly Daniels, the showband owner of the winner, Hazy Dawn, as he burst into 'When Irish Eyes Are Smiling' in the winners' enclosure.

Willie tells a revealing story concerning the preparation of Hazy Dawn, who had fallen uncharacteristically in her previous run. Instead of schooling her again, let alone extensively, he took the view that the opposite was best. He figured, she was already a great jumper of a fence, and as such she would be more careful on her next outing, so he did not school her at all – and it worked.

Two years later, he won the race again, this time on Mack's Friendly, bought on his behalf by his brother Tony from Davy McDonnell. The remarkable feature about this horse in winning the four-mile steeplechase was that he was by European champion sprinter Be Friendly. Be Friendly was owned by the sport's greatest and most mellifluous commentator, Sir Peter O'Sullevan. Born in County Kerry, Sir Peter was domiciled in England from a young age until his death at his London home in 2015, aged ninety-seven.

During the 1980s, Willie Mullins became Irish Champion Amateur Rider six times, and he also won the Liverpool Foxhunters – the 'amateurs' Grand National' – over the mighty Aintree fences on Ath Cliath.

He was also continuing to learn the training profession. He had a period away in Australia, learning much as an assistant trainer to Neville Beg. Then there was a spell with leading Irish flat trainer Jim Bolger, before becoming assistant to his father, Paddy, and then taking out a training licence on his own account. This was in 1988, with just four horses to train. Willie and Jackie, his wife of two years, moved into Closutton, bought by his father, which has been their home ever since.

Willie Mullins' first Cheltenham Festival winner as a trainer came in 1995 with Tourist Attraction, a bay mare owned by the North Kildare Racing Club, in the Supreme Novices' Hurdle at a price of 25-1. Tourist Attraction went on to produce a popular chaser called Pete The Feat, who won ten races in England, nine of them over fences.

The following year, Willie, who at this time still combined riding with training, took a gelding called Wither Or Which over for the Festival Bumper; the unfashionably bred gelding had been bought as an unbroken three-year-old at the Derby Sales. He showed huge talent at home, and also on his first racecourse appearance, when he won the bumper at the Leopardstown Christmas meeting by twenty lengths.

Next stop was Cheltenham – and proof that Willie Mullins' win the previous year had been no fluke, as Tourist Attraction's long price might have suggested.

Wither Or Which started second favourite in the Festival bumper. In the race he pulled hard, but ran on well to score by two lengths in the twenty-four-runner field. It was a huge fillip and defining moment in the young trainer's embryonic career.

One upshot was that he was offered a huge sum for the horse. He discussed it at length with Jackie. If they accepted, it would set them up financially.

'But,' Willie reasoned, 'we'll then become known as selling trainers – and this could be our break.'

Instead, they sold him for considerably less, but to stay in the yard. The buyers were Robert Sinclair and Noel O'Callaghan, while Willie himself kept a 'leg' in him.

The gamble paid off, with Wither Or Which winning his maiden hurdle and running in the 1996 Champion Hurdle, in which he was fifth of twenty.

It also showed potential owners that Willie had an eye for a relatively cheap, untried horse, and the ability to turn it into a racehorse, which gave them confidence to put horses in training with him.

We have been witnessing that eye and ability ever since.

* * *

Irish racing has been dominated by the Willie Mullins stable for a decade, and at the Cheltenham Festival for nearly as long. Why? Because success breeds success, and it has been thoroughly deserved. Not only was Willie the leading Irish trainer consecutively from 2007–08 to 2016–17, but at the end of the 2015–16 season, the UK championship went right to the wire. Willie was pipped on the line by Paul Nicholls, a remarkable feat given that the Irish trainer only sent a selection of horses over to England. It is a feat only previously achieved by one Irish trainer, and that was the trail-blazer Vincent O'Brien, back in the 1952–53 and 1953–54 seasons.

In 2001, Willie trained forty-four winners in Ireland, half the number of that year's champion trainer Noel Meade. That Christmas, Florida Pearl won the King George VI Chase in Kempton. In 2003, Willie sent eight horses over for the Cheltenham Festival.

In 2005, Hedgehunter won the Grand National, after which another steady stream of new owners came to Willie – and he was able to build a spacious extension to his home, christened the Hedgehunter wing.

Twelve years later, in 2015, he set a new Cheltenham record by training eight winners. In 2016, he despatched some sixty horses to run at Prestbury Park, another record.

Strength in depth (even in spite of the loss of some sixty Gigginstown Stud horses in the autumn of 2016), and continuous upgrading of facilities at Closutton, to the south of Carlow town, help his hand, but with upwards of 150 horses in training, it cannot be managed by one man alone. Willie is at the helm, and he runs a happy ship, but he could not manage without his right-hand men and women, all of whom carry out their responsibilities meticulously: his son, Patrick, is assistant trainer along with Davy Casey, who retired from race-riding in 2015 with two Cheltenham Festival winners to his name, along with big race wins in France and Ireland; a regular at Closutton since his teenage years, he already knew well how the yard ran. There are also the work riders, the yard managers, the head lad, the travelling head lad, the stable lads and lasses who muck out and groom daily, and plait and polish on race days, and not forgetting the invaluable office staff who undertake much of the administration from their stone-flagged office to the side of the house.

Huge travelling logistics are eased by specific delegation. Everyone knows his or her particular role, be it preparing the tack, the racing colours, and other minutiae, or a major role like transport, that all go together towards a successful end result.

When his father, the late, revered Paddy Mullins, was training from a relatively small site outside of Goresbridge, he said, you don't turn people away if you're full, because they won't come back – instead, you build more stables. He ended up with the largest NH stable in Ireland, with fifty horses. Today, Willie has three times that number, and Gordon Elliott is on even more at 200.

'When people are looking for a horse to put with me, they invariably ask for one that will get to Cheltenham,' says Willie. 'We always dream for just that. Owners like their horse to go there with a chance; they don't want to be twentieth of twenty-five.'

Occasionally this is decided on gut instinct, as when a horse has run below expectations in its pre-Cheltenham run but had the form before that.

He adds, 'Cheltenham has been good to us.'

Today, Willie has some fifty horses for Susannah Ricci, who, with her husband Rich, are loyal and very good owners.

Willie and Jackie Mullins are rightly proud of their son, Patrick. At six foot, it is remarkable that Patrick could make a success of race-riding at all, yet in 2012, he beat the record of seventy-two winners in a season, a record that had stood for ninety-seven years. For Billy Parkinson to have achieved that back in 1915 is truly remarkable. In 2012, Patrick notched winner number seventy-three with just two days of the year left, riding Zuzka at the Leopardstown Christmas Festival; and then he scored one more, so the record now stands at seventy-four. By this time, Patrick had emulated his father as a neat and powerful horseman. His record currently stands at eight amateur championships.

The stable jockey is Ruby Walsh, eleven times Irish Champion jockey, with more than 2,000 winners to his name, and eleven times champion jockey at the Cheltenham Festival. There, on fifty-six, he has ridden more winners than anyone else – in 2009 and 2016, he rode a record eight winners at the Festival.

Number two jockey at Closutton is the talented young Paul Townend, who has been on board a number of Grade 1 winners for the stable, and won the Irish jockeys championship in 2010–11.

Most aspiring jockeys dream of riding a Festival winner. In 2015, Paul Townend rode three: Glens Melody in the Mares' Hurdle, Irish Cavalier for trainer Rebecca Curtis in a handicap chase, and finally a 25-1 shot, Wicklow Brave in the concluding County Hurdle.

So, the Willie Mullins team has been built up along with the horses over the years, and what horses! (see a selection under Heroes and Heroines, page 91.)

* * *

A week, they say, is a long time in politics. In the summer of 2016, with almost daily resignations after the Brexit vote, even a day seemed a long time. For a decade, Willie Mullins and his splendid team, both human and equine, could do no wrong, and then – B-r-ooom.

In September 2016, some sixty Gigginstown Stud-owned horses were removed, widely reported as being due to training fees being increased (for the first time in ten years), and the O'Leary brothers, Michael and Eddie declining to agree to pay the increase. Empty stables are not a familiar sight at Closutton, and the ensuing vacancies were soon filled.

But worse was to follow. Part of the successful pattern of an increasing number of trainers is that horses are allowed a couple of hours or so at leisure daily in a paddock, usually with a familiar companion. Willie is an advocate of this, but one day in September 2016, the lad went to bring in Shaneshill and Vautour, lead ropes in his hand, as usual. He clipped the rope on to Shanehill's headcollar, but Vautour's foreleg was hanging limply. Somehow or other, the lovely, magnificent Vautour, with the main part of his career ahead of him, had broken a leg irreparably, almost certainly kicked by his companion. There was nothing for it but to put him down.

Look at him winning the 2016 Ryanair Chase in majestic style (see photograph, picture section 2, page 3), with such zest and talent. He was only seven years old, yet had already won at the Cheltenham Festival three times, including the 2014 Supreme Novices' Hurdle and the 2015 JLT Novices' Chase. He was widely touted as a future Cheltenham Gold Cup winner, and was ante-post second favourite behind Thistlecrack for the 2017 event.

He was owned by Rich and Susannah Ricci, for whom further disappointment waited around the corner – in January, their wonderful winners of the last two Champion Hurdles, Faugheen and Annie Power, were ruled out of the 2017 Festival with injuries, along with fancied Arkle Chase candidate Min.

After a sensational 2016 Cheltenham, Rich and Susannah Ricci certainly experienced the downside of racing. The loss of Vautour was tragic, and the injuries to the others were disappointing, to say the least. But the Riccis have such strength in numbers that they were still able to field a useful team at the 2017 Festival.

* * *

Willie Mullins, hard-working, accommodating, helpful, pleasant and smiling, is one of nature's true gentlemen, and he deserves his success. Another person who should not be forgotten is Maureen Mullins, matriarch of the Mullins clan, whose children and grandchildren have carved out successful lives, principally in horse racing. She was a brilliant and indispensable partner to Paddy Mullins, who died in 2010, aged ninety-one. Now aged eighty-seven, Maureen still adds a joyous and well-dressed touch in the winners' enclosure at Cheltenham, and a constant presence to her family.

Maureen has seen all five of her children and many of her grandchildren win races. She also won a race herself, on the only occasion she ever took part.

'She is very special,' says Willie. 'She's always there to support the clan and owners alike, especially when things have gone wrong. She's been there, and she understands.'

When winning owners at Cheltenham are invited to the hospitality box nearby to have a glass of champagne and watch a re-run of 'their' race, Maureen will be there to escort them if Willie and/or his wife Jackie have to go straight on to oversee their next runner.

MOUSE AND THE MONTH OF MARCH
– MOUSE MORRIS

Mouse Morris and Jonjo O'Neill lay alongside each other on trolleys in an American hospital corridor. Both had been injured riding in Camden, South Carolina – Mouse had sustained a broken leg, along with a number of other injuries. Both men were in great pain, but the system over there meant they would not be assisted until payment for treatment had first been handed over.

It was the beginning of the end of the riding career of Mouse Morris, whose highlights had included twice winning the (now Queen Mother) Champion Chase on board Skymas.

The fall in America happened when he was riding in the inaugural Colonial Cup in Camden, America's first international steeplechase, whose $100,000-dollar purse is only exceeded by the Grand National.

The race is just under three miles long, run over an inner and an outer loop, so that no one fence is jumped twice. The jumps are not the upright timber of the Maryland Hunt Cup, but bush-type fences, somewhat softer than English and Irish steeplechase fences.

It was first staged in 1970, with twenty-two runners, nine of them from five foreign countries. These included the Dan Moore-trained dual Gold Cup winner and Grand National hero L'Escargot, who finished fourth.

In the race, Mouse's horse was bumped into from behind at the first fence, sending his helpless rider spiralling over his head and hitting the ground as the horse's hooves trampled all over him.

'I broke everything,' he says, with a characteristic simplicity of words.

Mouse Morris left school at fourteen or fifteen to pursue his dream of being with racehorses. The story goes that he hid in a tree until it was too late for him to catch the ferry that would take him to another term at Ampleforth College in North Yorkshire.

'I was no good at school, and had to do something,' Mouse says, stubbing out another cigarette, in an ashtray already almost full by midmorning.

One suspects it was always going to be horseracing. It was in the blood. His father, Lord Killanin, is remembered for heading the Olympic Council of Ireland from 1950. He was President of the International Olympic Committee from 1972 until 1980, and was later unanimously elected Honorary Life President.

But horse-racing was a big interest. With family connections in Oughterard, Connemara, he was chairman of the Galway Race Committee for fifteen years from 1970 to 1985. In this time, he not only helped establish the Galway Festival that draws huge crowds to the Ballybrit course each summer, but also promoted Galway as a tourist destination. He was twice a Steward of the Irish Turf Club, which he joined in 1971, and once of the Irish National Hunt Committee.

It was to England that Mouse headed as a teenager, to Frenchie Nicholson, whose Prestbury stables were within sight of Cheltenham Racecourse.

Frenchie was a renowned tutor of future leading jockeys, both flat and jumping, and it was as an apprentice flat race jockey that Mouse Morris joined him, gaining a few rides on the flat while there.

He was still a teenager when, having switched to National Hunt as an amateur, he had his first ride at the Cheltenham Festival in 1969. This was the (now Fulke Walwyn/)Kim Muir Handicap Chase for amateur riders, and Mouse completed the course on a horse called Royal Cage. The race was won by Pride of Kentucky, trained by Edward Courage and ridden by Roger Charlton, the Derby-winning trainer based at Beckhampton, Wiltshire.

This race was just a taster for what was to come, memorably, both as a jockey and trainer, for Mouse Morris. As jockey Davy Russell said at a 2017 Cheltenham preview evening in Dublin, 'Mouse and the month of March are an extraordinary factor.'

His first Festival win came in the 1974 four-mile National Hunt Chase for amateur riders, on board Mr Midland, for one of the best and most durable Irish trainers Edward O'Grady, for whom it was also a first Festival win. Mouse turned professional not long after, and scored memorable dual riding successes in the top two-mile steeplechase on board Skymas in 1976 and 1977.

Ask Mouse what he felt about winning the Champion Chase twice, and he replies, 'It was grand.'

The accident in America pre-empted a change of direction for him.

'I wasn't going to train,' he says, 'but someone sent me a horse here to look after, and one thing led to another. Before that, I didn't know what I was going to do.'

'Here' is Everardsgrange, the rather posh-sounding name for his training establishment, a mile-and-a-half out of Fethard, County Tipperary.

It is more homely than its name suggests. On the way there, one might be held up by the turf train at a minor road crossing, as it chugs its way across the bog at barely a walking pace. There is a small engine both back and front – on the way out, the front train driver stops, alights and closes the road crossing gate; the train then chugs its way through, and when it stops again it's the turn of the driver in the rear engine to get out and open the gate, so that waiting vehicles can continue their journey.

Mouse Morris bought and renovated Everardsgrange when he began training in the early 1980s. To begin with, the house and its eighty acres housed a few cattle sheds and haybarns. These were converted to stables, and new ones have been built as and when the need arises. His gallops, both grass and all-weather, lie a little up the road on a slope.

He got off to a great start with one of the stars of the 1980s, Buck House. A contemporary of Dawn Run, he won the 1983 Supreme Novices' Hurdle. Three years later he won the Champion Chase, ridden by Tommy Carmody. Mouse Morris thus had success in the top two-mile chase both as a rider and a trainer, within a decade. This was the Festival at which Dawn Run won the Gold Cup. A month later, a special match race was arranged between the pair during the Punchestown Festival, over two-and-a-half miles, a compromise between her three-mile distance and Buck House's two. In a close contest, Dawn Run, ridden by Tony Mullins, ran out the winner. Within weeks, as previously noted, both superstars were dead, the mare killed by a fall in Auteuil, and Buck House from colic.

A sprinkling of success continued at the Festival at regular intervals for Mouse Morris. Horses trained by him were generally only entered if they had a good chance, and his reputation grew. In 1990, Trapper John won the Stayers' Hurdle, ridden by Charlie Swan.

Up until 2017, Mouse has sent out eight Cheltenham Festival winners, including the Gold Cup (see War Of Attrition, page 124), in addition to winning the 2016 Grand National at Aintree, with Rule The World at 33-1. Mouse has also won two Irish Grand Nationals, with Hear The Echo in 2008 and Rogue Angel in 2016. The latter made for an outstanding Aintree and Irish Grand National double.

To win the Grand National and the Irish National in the same year is an extraordinary feat, but it was tinged with exceptional sadness. Earlier that year, Mouse's elder son Christopher, known as Tiffer, had died from carbon monoxide poisoning while travelling in Argentina. He was thirty years old. A talented chef, he had been away looking at recipe ideas and seeing a bit of the world before a planned opening of his own restaurant in Dublin.

This was truly shattering news for Mouse, his younger son Jamie and Tiffer's mother, Shanny, married to Enda Bolger. The family went on to support Carbon Monoxide Awareness Week, doing a number of television appearances, newspaper features and radio interviews. The racing press were very good at promoting it as well, Mouse says.

'You can urge people to buy alarms,' he says, 'but they have to go out and buy it, you can't make them.'

He had one friend, however, who not only bought one for himself, but also for his mother. Just one week later, his mother's alarm went off while she was asleep. The Aga had become blocked, but thanks to the alarm, the mother was saved. The trouble with carbon monoxide is that it neither smells nor makes a noise, and if someone is sound asleep when it fills the air, it is a death sentence.

Mouse and his family will, naturally, keep promoting the alarms.

Mouse smiles and laughs a lot while chatting, wearing his well-worn baseball cap as usual, with its trademark mouse emblem, his hair flowing out from under it to around his shoulders. His faithful one-eyed greyhound–foxhound cross EJ is, as ever, by his side. Mouse's nickname came from his name, Michael Morris, becoming Mickey Mouse, and so Mouse he became.

His biggest smile is reserved for thoughts of his Gold Cup win with War Of Attrition for Gigginstown House Stud in 2006. 'That was my best moment, I suppose.'

He adds, 'I love Cheltenham, but I like to win the Gold Cup. Sometimes dreams are what keep us going.'

Each year, he takes a house within walking distance of the Cheltenham course. 'The owner allows me to smoke, and I can chill out,' he says. 'I look forward to going to Cheltenham every year. It's been a lucky place.'

A bronze trophy of War Of Attrition takes pride of place on his mantelpiece, with some of his favourite hunting photos nearby. Until recent years, Mouse loved nothing more than to cross the Tipperary country, and further afield, behind a pack of hounds, often in the company of his friends Demi O'Byrne and Timmy Hyde. He relished the big fences – the bigger the better – and the thrill of the chase, especially on board his favourite, a chestnut called Jerome.

Of the Gold Cup, he says it's a race he wants to win again.

'I've nothing obvious at the moment; it doesn't matter.'

He smiles again, and goes out to view some of his horses working. Maybe one of them will one day turn into another star.

'WE HAVE A GREAT LIFE' – HENRY DE BROMHEAD

At Knockeen, one takes a step back in time (after first gaining access through the automatic gates). A winding drive leads through fields to a fine house, with a typical Irish farmyard beyond it. A few horses' heads look out of old stables beside a large old stone haybarn.

The yard is totally unpretentious, much like the man at the helm. Henry De Bromhead is charming, friendly and welcoming. Outwardly laid-back, his attention to detail is meticulous, and nothing important is left undone.

On the day of my visit, it has been raining and the yard is muddy.

'We're going to do it up this year,' says the man in charge, but one feels that may have been said before. Priorities again.

His mobile phone seems glued to his ear. 'How did Vincent O'Brien manage without one?' he chuckles.

His father, Harry, sent out a Cheltenham Festival winner himself from this rustic yard – Fissure Seal, back in 1993. Henry wasn't planning to follow in his footsteps. He was mad about racing all right, but from a young age it was on the betting side. He was going to be an accountant, but he 'didn't really take to it'. Instead, he went to Coolmore and then Derrinstown, to acquaint himself with the stud side of the thoroughbred industry. Short-term spells in England saw him with Robert Alner and Ron Shaw as assistant trainer, followed by 'a fascinating' two years with Sir Mark Prestcott in Newmarket, and another two years with Coolmore in Australia and the USA. Then, in 1999, his father became unwell and was thinking of giving up. 'So I thought it was time to give it a go,' says Henry, whose licence dates from 2000.

'We've been lucky,' Henry says. He may have lost the horses belonging to Alan and Ann Potts at the beginning of the season, including Sizing John, but he gained a bunch of good Gigginstown ones that left Willie Mullins.

Nicole Kent, Henry De Bromhead's efficient racing secretary, 'loved Sizing John to bits. He was quirky but so easy to ride,' she tells me, as she hangs up sets of colours in the portacabin that serves as an office. There are some whiteboards on the wall, detailing different horses, and many photographs of glory days, including Queen Mother Champion Chase hero Sizing Europe. Alan Potts had been a long-time patron here, until moving most of his horses to Colin Tizzard in Somerset. A few, including Sizing John and Supasundae, went to Jessie Harrington at Moone, County Kildare, in the autumn of 2016.

The stand-out factor when visiting these stables, with Waterford city's skyline only a little to the north, is just how much each and every horse is clearly loved and cared for – no matter their ability, and no matter how many new barns have sprouted, barely visible from the original old yard. The horses' care is second to none. The new barns each have their own back door, leading to a woodchipped corral, and the horses can wander in and out at will. Every horse goes out into a grass paddock for a spell after work each day, unless it is too wet.

One of the Cheltenham hopefuls, Monalee (who has come either first or second in his six runs up to the the time of writing), has a goat with him – though they are standing in opposite corners of their corral. Thyestes Chase winner and Gold Cup possible Champagne West is sunbathing in the late February sun. He is 'an absolute gent, a bit like a hunter, big but so sweet,' says Nicole.

As we visit horse after horse, they all come to her. 'All our boys are used to lots of cuddles,' she says. This is apparent in their demeanour. None of them tries to push past, heading for the door, and none hangs back from attention.

Above: 'The Fly' in full flight. Hurricane Fly and Ruby Walsh on their way to victory in the 2013 Champion Hurdle.
Below: The Princess Royal stand was opened in November 2015. It offers a great view of the course, an almost tangible atmosphere, and a row of busy bookmakers in front.

In 2016, Annie Power (**above**) was supplemented for the Champion Hurdle, and won it in record time. Her trainer, Willie Mullins (**right**), transports his string of runners in a fleet of boxes (**below**).

Above: Vautour, seen winning the 2016 Ryanair Chase, had won three separate Cheltenham Festival races by the time he was seven. He was fancied for the 2017 Gold Cup, but was injured in a paddock accident at home.

Below: Barry Geraghty illustrates the ups and downs of being a jump jockey.

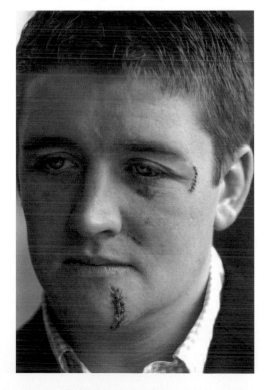

In 2017, all three Festival races for amateur riders were won by ladies, including (**above**) Lisa O'Neill on Tiger Roll for Ireland.

Left: Louise Cooper-Joyce, breeder of Hardy Eustace, and (**below left**) his trainer, the late Dessie Hughes.

Below centre: Simon Claisse and (**below right**) Edward Gillespie. Between them, they have many inside stories of the Irish at Cheltenham.

Above left: Legendary jockey and trainer Tommy Carberry, who died in 2017.
Above right: Queen of Cheltenham, Nina Carberry, on board On The Fringe in 2016, when they won their second Cheltenham Foxhunters Chase.
Below: Katie Walsh congratulates her brother Ruby, after his win in the 2017 Stayers' Hurdle. Katie, who finished sixth, has herself won two Festival races.

Above: Eight Irish fans ready for their day: (from left to right, standing) Rory Campbell, Ger Hennelly, Keith Neville, Liam Metcalfe, Gary Thornton, Nial Redmond, Paul Metcalfe and (seated) Hughie Kane.

Below left: Noel Fehily and children Niamh and Michael, with the Champion Hurdle trophy, 2017.

Below right: Trainer Pat Kelly and experienced jockey Davy Russell horse around after winning the Pertemps Network Final handicap hurdle with Presenting Percy.

Above: 2017 Champion Chase winner Special Tiara flanked by (left) trainer Henry De Bromhead, owner Sally Rowley-Williams, stable lad Stephen Dunphy and jockey Noel Fehily.

Below: Owner Graham Wylie with his Yorkhill, winner of the 2017 JLT Novices' Chase under jockey Ruby Walsh (centre).

Above: Lisa O'Neill holds aloft her trophy after winning the JT McNamara Chase in 2017.
Right: Jessie Harrington had an unforgettable 2017 Festival. She is seen here receiving the trophy for winning the Coral Cup with Supasundae.
Below: In 2003, her Moscow Flyer won the Champion Chase, seen here storming up to the finish.

Some Plan is another very friendly horse, as is the small Black Key, 'but he rides big'. Ordinary World is entered in the Arkle, and is 'a super ride'.

We come to Special Tiara, known as Mr T. He is 'an absolute gent until you put the saddle on, and then he's a monster'.

How so? I ask.

'He's crazy – a lunatic, fly-leaping all over the place, even at ten years old.'

It hasn't stopped him winning two Desert Orchid chases, though. He also entered the Queen Mother Champion Chase in 2017 for the fourth time (see page 219).

We come to Petit Mouchoir, known as Mushroom. He is at quite a short price for the Champion Hurdle.

He is 'an absolute poppet, a gent. He is keen on the gallops, but still a gent.'

Sub Lieutenant is entered for the Gold Cup, and here he is, mooching around a paddock in a turn-out rug.

Stellar Notion is a huge horse with very unusual white marking on his back legs. He is entered for the Grand National.

The stables are regularly tested for any bugs or viruses that might be lurking, and if any is found, they are thoroughly disinfected. All the stables have shredded paper bedding on top of rubber matting. The newer walkways are also covered in rubber. There is also a good-sized indoor sand arena, where horses can be loose-schooled over a steeplechase fence and the newer type of hurdle. They are sometimes let loose for a roll, which they love, and the arena is also handy in wet weather.

The horses have a spell on one of the three horse walkers before they go out for more strenuous exercise. Facilities include a three-furlong circular sand gallop, a woodchip gallop with a three-furlong uphill chute, a grass gallop, five uphill schooling fences and three flights of hurdles. But there is much more than these, good as they are, to the training at Knockeen. Three times a week, Rosemary Connors comes in to give dressage lessons to the horses, not only to make them supple and compliant, but also to produce a core strength.

All training methods differ, and Henry is not afraid to try different angles, while always paying attention to detail and keeping his horses healthy. His results have continually improved as he has climbed up the training tree. The first time he entered the top twenty Irish trainers was in 2009–10, and for the last three seasons he has finished third.

Cheltenham is the biggest meeting of the year, but one feels Henry takes it in his stride. Pre-Cheltenham, he is simply hoping to get his team over there in one piece; he has then done all he can. He is also a family man. With his wife, Heather, they have twins, Mia and Jack, aged eight, and Georgia, who is six.

'We have a great life of training,' says Henry, 'and if any of the children wanted to go into it, I wouldn't stop them. At the moment, the girls are keen, but Jack not so.'

However, there's no doubt that Jack will be jumping up and down with his sisters in front of the television, watching their father's horses, the moment they are home from school.

GOOD OLD DAYS, AND CAREFREE – COLM MURPHY

It is extraordinary to think that a youngish trainer, who has secured wins in both the Champion Hurdle and the Queen Mother Champion Chase, has relinquished his profession in the prime of life because he cannot make ends meet.

The news that Colm Murphy was retiring came out of the blue in September 2016, and sent shockwaves throughout the close-knit NH world, just as the new season was getting going.

Is it a sign of the times? Is Irish racing becoming dominated by two or three big stables? So much depends on having a stable star, and the bigger the stable the more likely it is to house one.

But Colm Murphy had two such stars. That is often when new owners clamour to become involved. Perhaps it was because the last big winner coincided with Ireland's long-drawn-out recession following the financial crash of 2008 that owners did not flock to his door. Whatever the reasons, he went through a long, lean period.

In recent times, Colm numbered Gigginstown House Stud, Alan and Ann Potts and JP McManus as owners, and had, in fact, produced a new star in Empire Of Dirt. Things were looking up.

Colm says, 'We had some exceptionally good owners. They come in all makes and shapes. There seems to be loyalty versus fashion now.'

Colm is a trained accountant, and the more he looked at recent figures, the more he realised it had become impossible to make ends meet. Pure pressure may also have had something to do with it. Willie Mullins and Gordon Elliott are busy, busy, busy men, virtually in perpetual motion. That is not for everyone, and some would prefer a slightly easier pace, while still working hard, gaining their share of winners and always dreaming of a new Cheltenham horse.

In his sixteen years of training near Killena, south of Gorey in County Wexford, Colm had much more than the two champions, Brave Inca and Big Zeb. His roll of honour also included the unbeaten mare Feathard Lady, who won seven races before being injured. She was saved for breeding, and her filly by Yeats, called Augusta Kate, foaled in 2011, has at the time of writing won five of her nine races.

After Feathard Lady's run of success, including the 2005 Christmas Hurdle at Leopardstown, the floodgates opened for Colm. At his zenith he had sixty-four boxes occupied.

'People might have thought to have one [good horse, i.e. Brave Inca] was lucky, but to have two shows you are doing something right.'

Quito De La Roque was another, owned by Gigginstown House Stud. He was a model chaser, extremely consistent throughout his career, until his last season when broken blood vessels caused his form to drop off. His last run was in the Grand National, but he never ran in Cheltenham. His career brought ten wins, several at Graded level, and six places from twenty-six runs.

The mare Voler La Vedette, bred and owned by Mrs Margaret Brophy, was another from the top drawer – she won thirteen of her twenty-seven races and placed in another nine, including two at the Festival. She finished third to Quevega in the Mares' Hurdle of 2010, missed the 2011 Festival, and then ran possibly the race of her life to run Big Bucks to one-and-three-quarter lengths in the World (Stayers') Hurdle of 2012, at a price of 20-1.

A few point-to-pointers, along with cattle and ponies, were part of growing up in Killena for Colm, his older brother John and younger sisters Catriona and Mary-Therese. They would go hunting on their ponies in the winter, and showjumping in the summer. When he left school, Colm attended college and trained as an accountant. He also used to ride out for Aidan O'Brien, who back in those days was a small NH trainer in Wexford with a big-profile horse in Istabraq. Aidan, discovering Colm's accountancy training, promptly persuaded him to work in his office in the afternoons, after riding out in the morning.

'They were good old days,' says Colm, 'and carefree. I was younger and had no worries. I swore I would never train horses.'

He was always buying and selling a few, though, and then had a permit to train (i.e. a restricted licence), and matters snowballed from there. One of the first horses he had with a full licence was Anvil Lord. He was lightly raced, suffering from a lot of leg trouble, but Colm produced wonders with him. Not only did he win three of his first four races, but in the first two there were thirty runners. The first time was at 20-1 in a maiden hurdle in Cork; next up was winning a handicap hurdle carrying only 9st 13lbs in Punchestown, at 12-1. Anvil Lord came third in a similar event at Gowran, and then, carrying almost a stone more than in his first handicap, he sluiced up again, this time in Navan. It was more than enough to put Colm on the map, and his professional career burgeoned from there.

Little did he know then that a future star, and one of the racing public's favourite heroes on both sides of the Irish Sea, was already stabled with him. Brave Inca's story is told on page 96.

Colm Murphy's stables are not completely bare now, although the block of four that had been the isolation stables by his house have their top doors boarded up. They are now home to his dogs – two boxers, Nancy and Bridie, and a terrier, Queenie. The main barn houses a number of youngsters that he is bringing on, and he is also breeding from a few mares. Now there are a few cattle around the fifty-eight-acre farm again – back to how it used to be when Colm was a boy.

Colm is taking his time. He might go back into accounting, his original qualification. Or he may stick to bringing on young horses, getting them to the point-to-point track and selling them on. Six months on from his decision to quit training, he had yet to set foot on a racecourse. But, he points out, he never went racing in the past either, unless he had a runner.

'Now was a good time to change if I was ever going to,' he says, 'otherwise I'd be another twenty or thirty years training, and if you can't make it pay …' His voice trails off.

It was a hard decision. He finally had another Cheltenham horse in Empire of Dirt, his last winner on the greatest jumping stage, in the 2016 Grade 3 handicap chase on St Patrick's Day, at 16-1.

Empire of Dirt moved on to Gordon Elliott, for whom he won the Troytown Handicap Chase at Navan from twenty-two rivals. He was just beaten in the Irish Gold Cup at Leopardstown in February 2017 by Sizing John – now that didn't turn out to be bad form. He held engagements in the Ryanair Chase and the Cheltenham Gold Cup, no less, for the 2017 Festival. In the event, he finished fourth, behind Un De Sceau, in the Ryanair.

For Colm, having had the 2016 Festival victory made it a bit easier for him to give up.

'I would hate to be going out feeling a failure. We ceased on *our* terms, rather than being forced out.'

But he admits it was hard telling his staff, six or seven lads and one girl, that he had to let them go. He kept just one on, Clyde Kennedy.

So, is the door a little bit open?

'Very much so, yes.' But then he adds quickly, 'but probably not to train.'

He adds, 'Of course I miss it; it's all I've ever done. When I had the good horses, it was viable.

'Cheltenham is our Olympics, and it's all you ever think of. It's a great place when you have a realistic chance, and the worst without. Cheltenham was a very, very lucky track for us, and I have fantastic memories, memories that can't be taken away. Most of what we ran there placed if it didn't win. I was lucky to have Brave Inca so early on. It's nice to have a CV to look back on.

'Racing in Ireland is so competitive, and the calibre of horses so good, as they are no longer being sold abroad. It's a numbers game now. There used to be predominantly syndicates, but now there are three or four big players. It's hard for syndicates and small owners not to accept big offers for promising horses, so there's a knock-on effect.

'Cheltenham is the one stage in racing that everyone knows about, and that's what everyone aims for.'

So, might he ever have a runner again?

'Never say never.'

Colm Murphy is certainly a loss to the Irish training ranks.

WORK HARD, PLAY HARD. AND GET THE WINNERS – GORDON ELLIOTT

'It's a numbers game – but we seem to be doing all right.' So says Gordon Elliott, with masterly understatement.

Look at the Irish stats to the end of February 2017: Horses from his stable had run a staggering 990 times, and produced 165 wins, meaning an average of one in six runners was a winner. The heir apparent to the title was, at this stage, fifteen winners ahead of Willie Mullins, whose horses had run 432 times (a staggering win:run rate of 1:2.8). The championship is decided on prize money and, at this time, Gordon Elliott led Willie Mullins by almost €400,000; both stables had topped €3 million. The outcome would hang on the spring festivals – and went right to the wire, when a treble, including two Grade Ones, on the fourth day of Punchestown, handed the title to Willie Mullins for a tenth consecutive year.

At the end of February 2017, Henry de Bromhead lay in third, with sixty-four wins from 363 runners, and €1,400,000 in prize money. Just seven Irish trainers had had runners in three figures at this stage – with Gordon Elliott close to four figures, or 1,000 runners! Look further down the table and there, on only fifty-two runs but with ten wins, lies the inimitable Ted Walsh. These are all enviable percentages of winners to runners.

Back in 2007–08, when Willie Mullins first topped the Irish trainers' championship, Gordon Elliott trained just six winners in Ireland – which was six more than the year before, although in that year he won the Grand National at Aintree. It is easy to say that victory in the world's most famous steeplechase kick-started his career, but it is much more than that. Gordon has in-depth racing knowledge and amateur rider experience, a great work ethic, an astute business brain and, above all, a Big Plan. And what is that? Winners, more winners, and to be champion trainer. Ask him what are his best days, and he replies, 'Winners.' And the worst? 'Injuries.' Not surprisingly, he especially remembers the 'amazing atmosphere' when he won the Cheltenham Gold Cup with Don Cossack in 2016.

He is quick to praise the staff around him, especially headman, right-hand man and very good friend Simon McGonagle, who has been with him since he started out in Trim. He also singles out his assistant trainers Ian Almond and Ollie Murphy, Zoe Winston in the office and Lisa O'Neill, amateur rider and part-timer in the office. Camilla Sharples is travelling head girl, and Mary Nugent is second travelling head girl. She loves the job, especially the frequent trips to the UK. Gordon employs some fifty work riders, and top jockeys such as Bryan Cooper regularly ride out and school also.

Senior work riders include former jockey Bobby McNally, a cousin of Gordon's. Bobby is particularly good at schooling young horses, and

Gordon takes close heed of his advice and feedback. Shane McCann is one of the longest-serving members of staff, and he mostly rode Don Cossack on exercise.

The main evening feeds are all prepared individually by one man, Simon McGonagle, a former point-to-point rider. He starts in the afternoon, as every single horse has its own feed, additives, and so on.

Ollie Murphy, assistant trainer, is due to begin training on his own, whereupon second assistant trainer Ian Almond will become first.

When his training numbers were getting bigger and bigger at the stables he rented at Capranny, near Trim, Gordon began looking around for a place to buy. The seventy-eight-acre farm at Cullentra House, Longwood in County Meath, had nothing more than a few farm buildings when Gordon bought it at auction in 2011 for €910,000, nearly €200,000 more than the guide – when Gordon Elliott wants something, he sets about getting it. After paying the weekly wages and the mortgage each month (he has no outside financial backer), whatever remains is ploughed back into improving and expanding the facilities. The result, within a few short years, is a massive training complex, with just about every conceivable training asset. The massive, American-style barns have mellow green rooves atop breeze-block walls, and rubber-matted aisles lie between the rows of stables. There is also a smaller courtyard block, and an isolation unit on the outskirts for up to six horses.

'We plough everything back in and now have everything we need,' Gordon says, 'it's as good as we could have it.'

It is low-lying land, but does include a slope, which appealed to Gordon with the Cheltenham finishing stretch in mind.

Nothing is left to chance. Monthly tests are carried out in the stables to check for bugs and viruses; thick blue pads, bearing the GE emblem, are worn under every saddle to protect tender backs from chafing; horses are turned out daily in wood-chipped yards. Horse-walkers are a 'thing' of Gordon's, and the horses also have an afternoon walk on them. Always uppermost in his mind is the next winner.

The massive sixty-by-forty-metre sand arena has already been doubled in size once, and looks set to be enlarged again. The horses go out in lots of forty to sixty at a time, and they all walk and trot in the arena every morning to warm up before they walk down rubbered paths and out to the choice of gallops at the bottom of the farm. It is wet land in this part of Meath, so the home gallops are made of all-weather materials such as sand and woodchips. To get the feeling of galloping on grass, horses are boxed up to Skryne, by the Hill of Tara, or to Punchestown or Fairyhouse racecourses.

There is a circular gallop, four furlongs round, as well as a straight gallop of six-and-a-half furlongs, a schooling lane, and a circular schooling lane inside the circular gallop; another gallop is planned. There is a stream down by the far side of the gallops, a 'natural spa' where the horses can paddle after work. Gordon has also recently installed an equine swimming pool, of which he is justifiably proud.

All the barns are named after local places – Agher, Moy, Clonmahon, and so on. Gordon is a local man, having grown up in Summerhill before first training from Capranny, outside Trim. From here, as a very new trainer, he sent out Silver Birch to win the 2007 Grand National.

Even the best-turned-out prizes are targeted, and more often than not they are won, a bonus for the lad or lass who 'leads up' the horse. After daily exercise, every horse is hosed down in a wash bay and then placed on one of seven horse walkers to dry off, but on the day before a horse races, the wash-down includes a full shampoo and set (all right, the set is the plaiting of the mane on race morning). The horses have a day off on Sunday, unless they are due to race in the coming week, in which case they are ridden.

'It's a lucky enough place,' says Gordon, 'but it's hard to have favourites with so many horses.'

He has a few though, including his first Festival winner, Chicago Grey. Owned by John Earls, Chicago Grey arrived with eight runs and four places, including a short-head second, already to his name. He promptly won three of his first four starts for Gordon and, memorably, won the four-mile National Hunt Chase for amateur riders at the 2011 Cheltenham Festival, patiently and skilfully ridden by Ireland's leading amateur, Derek O'Connor. It was Derek's first Festival win (as well as Gordon's), but in Ireland Derek O'Connor has scored an incredible record of more than 1,000 winners 'between the flags' (i.e. point-to-pointing).

It is not necessarily the best-known horses that are special to Gordon Elliott. He names Carlito Brigante, who won the 2011 Coral Cup Handicap Hurdle at Cheltenham, ridden by Davy Russell; and Toner D'Oudairies, a genuine work horse who twice ran in the Martin Pipe Conditional Jockeys' Hurdle at Cheltenham, finishing second once. He also nominates Clarcam – still only seven years old, he has run thirty-nine times, won eight and placed in twelve races not all that far from the top echelons.

'He's not the greatest, but he's a real tryer,' says Gordon.

He also selects Roi Du Mee, who retired at the end of 2016 having won thirteen chases and placed in another eleven. He was also a favourite of the O'Learys, and will see out the rest of his days at their Gigginstown Stud, along with War Of Attrition and Grand National hero Rule The World. He was one of those little horses with a big heart, and was much loved throughout the Elliott yard.

Gordon told the *Racing Post*, 'He was the first real Grade 1 horse that I trained, and I owe him an awful lot. He wasn't the biggest, but he had a massive heart.'

Eddie O'Leary, Michael's brother and racing manager, says, 'Michael is not the most sentimental man, but this horse made him sentimental, as he over-achieved all of his life and won races he shouldn't have. He had a heart that surpassed his ability.'

We walk round the whole huge complex. Only the office is yet to be made, in one remaining old barn, and until then Zoe Winston and her team's facility is a portacabin, with another next door as the canteen. Unsurprisingly, the horses' requirements have come first. Zoe is shadowed by a grey-coloured Great Dane called, appropriately, Shadow, who was bought by Gordon to celebrate Don Cossack's Gold Cup win. When he is not with her, he is at Gordon's side, in his kitchen or around the complex. Zoe and her husband, second head lad John Winston, live in Capranny House, and Gordon has a newly built house next door.

Gordon has the country's major players as owners, but those with lighter purses are not left out, and Zoe is responsible for running the Gordon Elliott Racing Club. In typical Gordon Elliott style, the club's four horses run not only anywhere in Ireland, but also across the whole of the UK. Prize money is split equally between club members, and members enjoy a couple of pre-arranged visits to the yard to watch not just their horses work, but the stable stars, too. Who knows? One of their horses may turn out to be a star. Hopes and dreams keep racing alive, and the approximately £9 per week (£500 per year) that club members pay is hugely more affordable than the £350 or so per week that individual owners pay per horse.

Occasionally, stable tours are conducted on quiet days, 'as we don't want anything to disrupt the daily running of the yard,' says Zoe. 'Sometimes these will be for people who have won a tour by raffle (we give away lots of tours to charity events), or people who have called and asked for their relative's birthday. We have syndicate and Racing Club open mornings perhaps twice a season, but if members want to come along at any time they are welcome, as long as it is a suitable day (i.e. not over Cheltenham, etc!)'

When, in September 2016, Michael O'Leary took away all sixty of the horses that he had with Willie Mullins, eighteen of them went to Gordon Elliott. Gordon already had fifty-nine horses for Gigginstown, and as I write he trains some seventy-seven for them.

He says, 'They are results-based owners, and luckily we are getting results.' That numbers game again.

One of the earliest means by which he gained wins that other Irish trainers seldom did was by sending horses to Scotland, England and Wales to race. This was not just for the big races, but also especially for moderate handicaps, novice hurdles (which have many entries liable to be balloted out at declaration stage in Ireland) and humble sellers (which are not run in Ireland). Part of the pull was to find better ground, as most Irish tracks are regularly soft to heavy. Gordon had clearly learned from his time with Martin Pipe in the Somerset trainer's years of innovation, and this was one that Gordon sussed out for himself, looking 'outside of the box'. This placing of horses, often avoiding the top trainers and going for modest races, has served him well. He has also been canny at buying already exposed horses and producing results. Up until 2015, at Perth he had achieved 124 winners from 415 runners (a win rate of one in 3.3 runs), and Downpatrick, an undulating 'switchback' course in Northern Ireland, with fifty-four winners from 269 runners. Neither track would be considered 'fashionable'.

Perhaps surprisingly, horses did not feature in Gordon's younger childhood, other than visits to local point-to-points with his non-horsey parents. One day, however, they sent young Gordon with a message for Martin Lynch, and while there he found himself asked to hose a horse's leg. Before he knew it, he was there every day after school, and being taught to ride by Martin's wife, Suzanne. By the time he was a teenager, he spent every spare moment with trainer Tony Martin, and had a few rides in point-to-points. He left school early, before he was chucked out, and went on to ride a couple of hundred winners, including a winner from just half-a-dozen rides for Martin Pipe. He twice rode at Cheltenham's Open meeting in November, but, from a young age, he looked longingly at the Festival. With rising weight and dodgy shoulders, it was only the year before the Grand National win that Gordon gave up race riding.

Of all his many feats, one of the most admirable has to be that he rode in the Maryland Hunt Cup, the daunting fixed-timber race, with some of the fences standing five feet high. He finished second, on a horse called Rosbrian. To jump those at racing pace on a thoroughbred takes nerve. There is no shortage of that in Gordon Elliott.

On to Cheltenham 2017. Gordon Elliott is Champion Festival Trainer. Just ten years have gone by since Silver Birch won the Grand National for Gordon in his first season as a trainer. The liquid celebrations lasted long into the night and over the next few days. Before that auspicious day at Aintree, he had trained just three winners – two in Perth, Scotland, and one in the West Country, at Newton Abbott. His first in his home country came a few weeks later, at the start of the new season, in Kilbeggan in the heart of County Westmeath.

Probably the biggest factor behind Silver Birch's Grand National victory was that he had left a big English stable for what was then a small one and, crucially, Gordon Elliott used to take him hunting. The horse relished heading out across the Meath countryside behind the Ward Union hounds, across huge double banks and ditches.

A decade on from Silver Birch, Gordon Elliott may have Ireland's biggest stable, but one thing has not changed: he likes nothing more than a good night out celebrating a big win. He loves his visits to Cheltenham, where he stays 'with a good bunch of lads' in The Butts, a group of holiday cottages within walking distance of the racecourse.

He is on the course by 7.30am, watching his charges work. Then he sees to the necessary declarations, and after breakfast it's time to go racing.

There is more pressure at Cheltenham, he concedes, 'with everyone watching, but I enjoy it, and I've got good staff, owners and horses.

'I enjoy the night life. We work hard during the day, and afterwards we go into the town for a few drinks.'

Work hard, play hard, that's the maxim. And get the winners.

'I THINK YOU CAN HAVE IT IF YOU WANT IT' – JONJO O'NEILL

Ask Jonjo O'Neill for his most memorable moment at Cheltenham and the answer, inevitably, is, 'Dawn Run. It was a day in a lifetime. It could never happen again.'

The way the pair fought back up the run-in to win the 1986 Gold Cup, after staring at defeat when she was overtaken going into the last fence, is an indelible part of Irish folklore, legendary throughout the world of jumping and sport beyond. Watch the recording for the umpteenth time and she still *can't* get up to win – but she did.

But, surprisingly, the prospective ride on Dawn Run was *not* what Jonjo was most looking forward to that day. Indeed, until a few short weeks before, he did not think he would have the ride, and the way he was feeling, he hardly cared. In fact, having had a couple of distinctly hairy schooling sessions on Dawn Run at home in Doninga, County Kilkenny, under the scrutiny of trainer Paddy Mullins (a proposed race-ride at Punchestown having been snowed off), Jonjo could not understand why she was running in the Gold Cup at all, let alone as favourite. The Gold Cup was Jonjo's first public appearance on her in a chase, although he had been aboard for five hurdle races. Four of these were wins, including the 1984 Champion Hurdle.

No, what was uppermost in Jonjo's mind before that March day in 1986 was his ride in the last race of the Festival, the County Handicap Hurdle. He had been anticipating it with relish for months. This was what was keeping him going, because, since being brought down in a pile-up in a hurdle race at Kelso, he had been feeling decidedly ill. So ill, in fact, that he was seriously considering quitting the saddle. But he was determined to win that race first.

He recalls clearly the fall that led to him feeling so poorly: three of them were in single file – Chris Grant, Phil Tuck and then him. The leader fell and brought down the other two. But, sore as he was, Jonjo asked a friend, Gordon Smith, to drive him to Ascot, for rides on Just Alec and Jobroke. Kevin Mooney substituted for him on the first ride, but Jonjo felt well enough for the next. The horse's trainer, Peter Easterby, at home near Malton in North Yorkshire, was sending messages that he shouldn't ride.

'Tell him you can't find me,' Jonjo said to Gordon Smith. He changed and weighed out, so that it was too late to change the jockey. The pair won 'cosily' and, in spite of his increasing tiredness and aching, it furthered his incentive to keep going for Cheltenham. Jobroke would win the County Hurdle, of that he was sure. The gelding had been 'laid out' for the race by trainer Peter Easterby, owner Colonel Dick Warden and Jonjo himself, and was set to carry only ten stone three pounds.

Come the day, Jonjo won the epic Gold Cup on Dawn Run. The euphoria of the Irish, and indeed all of those in attendance, was tangible, almost as it had been for her Champion Hurdle success two years earlier. On that occasion, the fans pouring into the winners' enclosure tried to tear memorabilia from the helpless jockey. Jonjo hung on to his number cloth and breast girth as fans had him literally off his legs, trying to pull them off him on the way to the weighing room. He spent the whole of those twenty yards clutching on to the items for dear life – without them at weigh-in, Dawn Run would be disqualified. As racing author Tim Richards so cogently noted, in Jonjo's words in his 1985 autobiography, 'The admiring thousands stood shoulder to shoulder above us [as they rode in] and as I raised my arm with a wave of appreciation before I dismounted, the response was instantaneous …' But mob rule nearly spoiled the party; many had infiltrated the enclosure, and 'as about twenty of them surrounded me and cut me off from the main, noisy, admiring crowd, which numbered thousands … Panic nearly set in as I fought against a sea of people pressing from all sides. My number cloth slid from under my saddle and my breastgirth was being tugged from my arm, which was laden with tack. Without these vital pieces of equipment I would fail to pass the eagle-eyed clerk of the scales, George Gregory, at the weigh in and he would object to the stewards, who, in turn, would have no option but to do the unthinkable and disqualify Dawn Run. … I was on my own at the heart of an over-excited mob … the number cloth was being wrenched from me by a souvenir hunter … no sooner had that battle been won (thanks to another unknown Irishman) than I realised someone else was tugging at my breastgirth. … I called on all my reserves of strength for one last wrench.'

Today, the paddock area is strictly patrolled. Such scenes, no matter their misguided enthusiasm, are nearly a thing of the past (although an occasional fan has been known to get through).

Two years later, when Dawn Run achieved the incredible Champion Hurdle/Gold Cup double, it cannot be said that security had yet reached the level of today. However, while the scenes were ecstatic and the enthusiasm electric, there was not the real danger to the race result that there had been after the Champion Hurdle.

The Gold Cup victory was not only Jonjo's career highlight, but also one of the most memorable moments in the sport's then 232-year history.

For the record, Jonjo then duly signed off on his Cheltenham riding career with exactly the win he had coveted, on Jobroke in the last race of the day.

Barely six weeks later, he was diagnosed with cancer.

Jonjo did not come the pony-racing/point-to-pointing route into racing, but via hunting. Once he had his first pony, Dolly – a £27.2s.0d purchase from Tullow fair – he lived for the sport, following the Duhallow hounds in County Cork. He admired the style and riding aplomb of Anne, Duchess of Westminster, and he hero-worshipped the McLernon, Harding and Murphy families, all steeped in National Hunt racing, who took him to local point-to-points. At the end of a long day's hunting, with Jonjo quite lost, one of them would point him in the direction of home, and off he would set, dusk gathering. When he wasn't hunting with the Duhallow, he went out with a local harrier pack on a Sunday. He just loved hunting, and the craic that accompanied it. It also gave him a good eye across country, and a secure seat, both crucial in jump racing.

On one such day, the whole hunt stopped at a cottage, tied up their horses outside, and watched a crackly black-and-white transmission of the 1966 Cheltenham Gold Cup. The Duchess's Arkle, trained by Tom Dreaper, scored his third consecutive victory under Pat Taaffe, in spite of demolishing the fence at half way. This was Jonjo's introduction to Cheltenham, and he determined to get there one day. His original racing inspiration had come three years earlier, when nineteen-year-old Pat Buckley steered Ayala to victory in the Grand National. From watching those two races, Jonjo's destiny was decided.

He began riding out for Chris Major's private trainer Donald Reid (whose son, Fred, became a well-known Lambourn farrier) in nearby Mallow, and stayed there once he had left school. The trainer returned to England and, with Jonjo weighing barely six stone, he was apprenticed to an extremely tough flat trainer on The Curragh.

With that behind him, and weight increasing, jumping beckoned. He got one or two moderate rides, and won on Irish Painter at Downpatrick for trainer Mick Connolly. Then a spare ride came along, without any high hopes, that was to set him upward on his chosen path. The owner was Mrs Guy Sharrick, the horse was Mount Royale and it was his first time over fences, in Navan. The pair won – and England beckoned.

Jonjo moved to Gordon Richards' stable in Greystock Castle, Penrith, where 'Big' Ron Barry was stable jockey, and Cumbria remained his home for many years. Jonjo became champion conditional jockey, and then a top senior one, during the five years he was there, but with the injuries that he also suffered, his career was in jeopardy more than once. When the first leg break happened, on a horse called Night Affair at Teesside early in 1975, he could see his bone sticking out through his boot 'like a nail'. He had broken his tibia and fibula, the main lower leg bones, as well as his knee.

By the time he broke his tib and fib for a second time, riding at Bangor in October 1980, he was already champion jockey. With superlative Cheltenham rides in the offing – tempting morsels like Sea Pigeon to retain the Champion Hurdle, and former champion hurdler Night Nurse who he was convinced would win the Gold Cup – he wanted to be the man on board. His impatience cost him those rides – and almost lost him his leg. He tried riding out long before his ever-helpful surgeon said he should, and the not-yet mended leg, unable to take the strain, now resembled shards. Jonjo ended up under the knife in a Swiss clinic, his surgeon in attendance. On waking up, he did not know whether or not his leg had been amputated. It had been touch-and-go.

For the record, Sea Pigeon won the Champion again, in the hands of John Francome, and Night Nurse finished second. Little could Jonjo guess then that he would still be the man to steer home the first and, so far, only winner of both the Champion Hurdle and Gold Cup.

In the late 1970s, Jonjo had made the brave decision to turn freelance. Without a top stable behind him, his career might have been doomed, but Jonjo's riding skills, established across the County Cork countryside and now honed to become one of the best and strongest of jump jockeys, meant his services were snapped up, and he enjoyed astonishing success. In 1977–78, he not only scored the fastest 100 winners, but continued to a then-record 149 winners in one season.

He won the 1979 Cheltenham Gold Cup on Alverton, and followed up with Champion Hurdle wins in 1980 on Sea Pigeon and in 1984 on Dawn Run.

After the phenomenal 1986 Gold Cup victory with Dawn Run, Jonjo was turning his thoughts to training – but instead it was to be weeks of chemotherapy and all the attendant travails of serious illness. He remains convinced that the fall in Scotland caused the onset of cancer.

Before the illness, he had twenty-four horses for training; when he recovered, there were two. He swiftly and determinedly set about re-establishing Ivy House, Penrith, which he had bought a couple of years earlier, into as good a training establishment as was possible. He sank his own money into Ivy House, set in lovely Lakeland countryside, and installed virtually all the facilities that are enjoyed by Jackdaws today. Through riding as a freelance, he had seen many different stables, all with their own unique ways of training, yet all of which produced winners. It meant he was open to a wide range of ideas, and he installed many excellent facilities at Ivy House, including an equine swimming pool. By the early 1990s, he had achieved all that was possible there, including a winner on the Flat at Royal Ascot. But there was one drawback: the big owners and chief race meetings were all based in the southern counties. The money was not in the North. If he was to attract more owners, he would have to move South.

He looked at a number of places, and at one time was in serious discussion with Edward Gillespie, then Cheltenham's CEO, about creating a training establishment in the middle of the racecourse, in the helicopter landing field.

When Jonjo first heard of Jackdaws Castle, he had no intention of even viewing it, let alone moving there. This was because it was owned by someone else, who might therefore be calling the tunes and, having been freelance for so long, Jonjo was not at all sure he could work as a salaried trainer.

'I had been my own boss for so long, I didn't think I could work for someone else again.'

It was his now-wife, Jacki, from nearby Tewkesbury, who persuaded him to at least take a look.

Jackdaws Castle sits in the lofty Cotswolds, on wonderful old, well-drained soil above Stanton Hill, not far from Stow-on-the-Wold (and a mere twelve miles from Cheltenham racecourse). From the car park beside the Plough Inn at Ford, the casual observer can watch a string of bay horses, divided into five groups of four and all wearing number cloths, trotting past. They turn back, cantering up the long, steady hill, followed by a smart white BMW, the horses' trainer at the wheel, a little brown-and-white terrier beside him.

The trainer will then see them settled in, return to the hub for declarations and staff meetings, and snatch a bacon butty in the 'owners room'. Overlooking Number 1 yard, it is surrounded by trophies, photographs, three or four televisions replaying races, and racks of champagne flutes ready for entertaining. Outside, three yards house 110 or so horses. There is a solarium, a therapy bay, horse walkers, wash-down bays, an indoor school and an equine swimming pool. Out on the 500 acres, there are three grass gallops and two Polytrack ones.

Jackdaws' previous incumbent had been David 'the Duke' Nicholson, so it was already well established – and was ripe for further improvement. Jonjo loved it on first sight, but the ownership niggle remained. Might the landlord sell it? Indeed, he might.

What followed could have been straight out of an Irish sit-com. There was no way Jonjo could buy it. But there was one very special Irishman, for whom Jonjo not only rode but for whom he also had huge respect, who could: Ireland's leading owner and legendary gambler JP McManus. Jonjo rang him and described it.

At a later point, he rang him again on some pretext, and JP told him he was currently in London.

'So am I,' fibbed Jonjo from his Cumbrian home, and arranged to see JP at his hotel for breakfast in the morning.

So Jonjo caught the last train out of Carlisle bound for London. Arriving in the early hours, he tramped the streets, trying to stay awake until it was time for his appointment.

During breakfast, conversation roamed over a broad range – almost anything, in fact, except Jackdaws.

Finally, as Jonjo was leaving, JP said nonchalantly, 'By the way, whatever happened to that place in Gloucestershire?'

'Oh, yes, Jackdaws,' Jonjo replied, equally coolly. 'I think you can have it if you want it.'

The rest, as they say, is history. Jonjo trained 100 winners in his first full season at Jackdaws, 2001–02, making him the only man to have scored 100 winners both as a jockey and as a trainer. He repeated the feat the following season; and in 2003, he was leading trainer at the Cheltenham Festival, with a winner on each of the three days.

In 2005, Clan Royal was leading and looked like winning the Grand National at Aintree for the trio of JP McManus, Jonjo O'Neill and AP McCoy, until he was carried out by a loose horse at Becher's second time. The ever-competitive AP told Jonjo afterwards that it was a 'disaster'.

'No,' Jonjo replied, 'disaster is when you're lying in hospital waiting for the doctor to come and tell you whether you are going to live or die.'

That put it into perspective for AP. He told the new ITV racing team in a feature about Jonjo in January 2017, 'That made me change from then on.'

In 2010, Jonjo did train the winner of the Grand National, Don't Push It. He had two runners, both for JP, and JP's retained jockey AP McCoy had first choice. He was hankering towards the other one, Can't Buy Time, but Jonjo strongly, and correctly, advised Don't Push It. As a result, the Ulsterman and twenty-times Champion jockey finally achieved Grand National success, at his fifteenth attempt.

In 2012, the same team won the Cheltenham Gold Cup with Synchronised, and the 2013–14 season was Jonjo's most successful so far, winning over £1.5 million in prize money. For the fifth time in twelve years, he trained three winners at the Festival – Holywell, Taquin Du Seuil and More Of That, who won the Ladbrokes World Hurdle. His other winners included Johns Spirit in the Paddy Power Gold Cup and Shutthefrontdoor in the Irish Grand National.

Jonjo has now been in racing for fifty years, and his ambition and pursuit of excellence burn as strong as ever.

'I want to be champion trainer. We'll get there,' he says simply.

He has the know-how and the facilities; all he needs now is the ammunition.

About a third of his yard will have Cheltenham entries, and about a third will be owned by JP McManus, a number of these overlapping.

Cheltenham remains the theatre where he wants to succeed more than any other. As he told Brian Viner in an *Independent* interview, 'The magic of Cheltenham is very hard to explain ... From now on I will be excited every morning. It's the ultimate in jump racing. As soon as you're done with Christmas, then, like everybody else in this game, all you're interested in is Cheltenham.'

CHAPTER 7

AS GOOD
AS THEY GET
– JOCKEYS

GOLD AND A MULTITUDE OF RUBIES

Ruby Walsh could be called the elder statesman and ambassador of Irish jockeys. Nowhere is he more dominant than at Cheltenham, where he is held in high regard by the upper echelons of the management, owners, trainers, fellow jockeys and an adoring public alike.

It is not just the wins, but the sheer experience that he brings to his craft. He will support an injured jockey, fighting his corner if need be, and occasionally remonstrate with a rookie jockey (down at the start, for instance). He is always willing to lend a hand, be it for fellow jockeys or for the reputation of the sport in general. There was a time at a fairly recent Cheltenham Festival that a sign had been wrongly erected mid-race; Ruby was on his feet, having fallen earlier, and he ran out to signal the correct way to go to the remaining jockeys.

'He was fully supportive in the subsequent enquiry [into the wrongly-placed sign],' says Simon Claisse, Cheltenham's Clerk of the Course. 'Anyone can make a mistake, and Ruby was absolutely brilliant.'

Ruby's injuries have been truly dreadful, including a ruptured spleen at the 2010 Cheltenham Festival. In addition, at various times, the crushed vertebrae, concussion and many broken and dislocated bones would leave lesser mortals wondering why on earth a jockey should keep coming back for more. But one look at Ruby's face when he steers home an important winner, and there is the answer.

He has been quoted with particularly withering remarks about footballers faking injuries. He told the *Mail Online* in 2013, 'You're either hurt or you're not. When you deal in a sport where serious injuries take place, to see someone feign injury is actually a little bit revolting.

'I can't watch football, because there is no point. They're not playing football, they are acting, and they are bad actors at that.'

Walsh described jump jockeys as 'fair, tough and honest', and revealed that the mental side of getting hurt is often harder to recover from.

Racing is in Ruby's blood. In fact, his blood must be rainbow-coloured, so steeped is his breeding in this colourful sport.

Ruby Walsh was born to horsemanship and racing, and not only through his father Ted, top amateur jockey with four Festival wins (today, Ruby achieves more than four per Festival and, in 2017, actually achieved four in one day). Ted is also a canny trainer and TV racing pundit. It goes back to Ted's father, also Ruby. He was christened Edward, but was nicknamed Ruby because of his golden, curly hair.

Ruby senior, the youngest of nine children, grew up in County Cork. He ran the family pub and farmed, as well as keeping a horse or two, riding in a few point-to-points, and sourcing a regular supply of troop horses. He took the family to America for a spell, following glowing reports from older brothers, but didn't like it. He returned to set up as a racehorse trainer in the Phoenix Park, Dublin. On his death in 1990, Ted Walsh took over the licence, and in due course moved to Kill, County Kildare, from where he still trains. There Ruby and his siblings grew up with Ted and their mother, Helen: top-class amateur jockey Katie; rugby-loving Ted junior, married to ace amateur rider Nina Carberry; and Jennifer, Ruby's highly efficient agent.

Ruby Walsh is as good as they get. He has ridden more Grade 1 winners than any other NH jockey worldwide; and nowhere is he better than at Cheltenham. His first Festival win came in 1998, in the Bumper, on Alexander Banquet, whose dam was by Monksfield, hero of the 1978 and 1979 Champion Hurdles.

Since then, Ruby Walsh has ridden more Festival winners than any other jockey – fifty-six to date (2017). These wins have included two Gold Cups on Kauto Star; three Queen Mother Champion Chases (Azertyuiop and Master Minded twice); and the Champion Hurdle four times (on Hurricane Fly twice, as well as Faugheen and Annie Power).

In 2010, he achieved the record for most winners at the Festival. In both 2009 and 2016, he rode seven Festival winners. And he has been the leading jockey at the Festival eleven times in the fourteen years between 2004 and 2017.

From 2002 to 2013, Ruby Walsh was based in England, riding as first jockey to champion trainer Paul Nicholls. He got home to Ireland only occasionally, mainly for the Sunday racing, which is much more of a feature in Ireland than in England. Willie Mullins was delighted to have Ruby back. Ruby first began working for Willie at seventeen years old, and rates him a friend more than a boss. In races, Willie leaves Ruby to his own tactics, which he can then alter as a race unfolds.

The 2017 Festival was an unusual one for the partnership. After two blank initial days (and winnerless again for Ruby on the final day), it was hard to imagine he would end up as top jockey again. Yet an incredible four-timer on the third day once more put him into the record books.

A KNIGHT IN RACING ARMOUR – SIR AP MCCOY

It was at a point-to-point in Wexford that the late English trainer Toby Balding first spotted the talents of an Ulster amateur, one Anthony – AP – McCoy. 'He was accomplished, rode with style, and when speaking to him, he looked one straight in the eye,' recalled Toby some years later.

So, AP joined the long list of future top jockeys (Adrian Maguire among them) that gained their grounding with Toby, as he joined his Hampshire stable as conditional jockey. Before that, AP, from Money-glass in County Antrim, had learnt much from the late Billy Rock, who was his training idol, and then even more with Jim Bolger on the flat, where he rode nine winners. Soon, he grew too tall, and it was clear he would be better off jumping.

In no time at Toby Balding's, he had ridden out his conditional jockey's claim. He won the Conditional Jockeys' title with a record seventy-four wins. This was just a foretaste of what was to come: for the next twenty consecutive years, he was Champion NH jockey, until his retirement in 2015.

With wins on such as Beech Road and Viking Flagship, and his 1997 Cheltenham double of Mr Mulligan in the Gold Cup and Make A Stand in the Champion Hurdle, he had all too soon 'outgrown' Toby's stable, too, good though it was. He now joined Martin Pipe.

To quote Toby Balding again, AP was 'a product of the modern style, pure jockeyship'.

Add to that utter commitment and determination, total tunnel vision, and an exceptionally strong style, and we have the makings of one of the all-time great champions, to many the best ever.

The glory years with Martin Pipe followed. Year after year, the pair deservedly won the jockeys' and trainers' championships. Then McCoy moved to Jonjo O'Neill, at JP McManus' Jackdaws Castle in Gloucestershire, from which base he continued to head the jockeys' table.

Some horses thrived on AP's style, and Brave Inca was a perfect example. 'A match made in heaven' was one description of their heroic Smurfit Kappa Champion Hurdle in 2006. This was the middle of three Champion Hurdle wins for AP; the other two were Make A Stand in 1997 and Binocular in 2010.

He also won two Gold Cups – on Mr Mulligan in 1997 and Synchonised in 2012 – and one Queen Mother, on Edredon Bleu in 2000, in a total of thirty-one Festival wins.

In February 2015, AP signalled his intention to retire at the conclusion of the 2014–15 season. He announced it live on television, as he rode back in from a dramatic victory in the Game Spirit Chase at Newbury, in which the reigning two-mile champion chaser Sire de Grugy had blundered and given his jockey no chance of staying on board.

It was shock news, but one had to admire this greatest of all NH jockeys all the more for doing it his way. I don't know AP personally, but sent a note of congratulations after he notched his four-thousandth winner at Towcester on November 7 2013. It never occurred to me that there would be a reply, but he sent a round-robin card. I think of the number of letters sent to people from whom at least some sort of acknowledgment could – should – have been received, and yet this exceptional man did so when it definitely wasn't called for. He is probably the greatest NH jockey – indeed sportsman – Britain or Ireland is ever likely to produce. In the New Year Honours of 2016, he deservedly become only the second jockey ever, after flat jockey Sir Gordon Richards, to be knighted.

Incidentally, for those who weren't at Newbury or watching on the telly, AP rode in the next race after announcing his retirement – and fell at the first. Unscathed, he travelled to Ireland, where he won on Sort It Out and then, to tumultuous applause and admiration, landed the Hennessy Gold Cup on JP McManus' Carlingford Lough.

A FESTIVAL FAVOURITE – BARRY GERAGHTY

In the summer of 2015, Barry Geraghty was confirmed as number one jockey for JP McManus, following the retirement of AP McCoy. It meant relinquishing his position as first jockey to Nicky Henderson, but it enabled him to spend more time with his wife, Paula, and young family at home in Ratoath, County Meath, especially on week days; his riding commitments in England are mainly on Saturdays.

Barry has ridden more than 1,000 winners, including the Grand National on Monty's Pass and many at the Cheltenham Festival. He was leading jockey there in 2003, with five winners, and he has won the Queen Mother Champion Chase five times. Until 2017, when he missed the Festival through injury, Barry had won at least one race at the Festival from 2002 to 2016.

One of six children of Tucker and Bea Geraghty, Barry's childhood revolved around ponies (his mother ran a riding school), hunting with the Ward Union and generally laying the foundations for a career as a jockey. Much of his early career was moulded by Jessie Harrington, for whom he won the Midlands National at the age of nineteen. That led to his great association with Moscow Flyer (see page 108). He won the 2009 Champion Hurdle on Punjabi, meaning that he had won all four of the Championship races.

Barry's Cheltenham Festival winners are:

2002 – Arkle Challenge Trophy, Moscow Flyer

2003 – William Hill Trophy, Youlneverwalkalone; Pertemps Final, Inching Closer; Queen Mother Champion Chase, Moscow Flyer; Triumph Hurdle, Spectroscope; and County Hurdle, Spirit Leader

2004 – Stayers' Hurdle, Iris' Gift

2005 – Queen Mother Champion Chase, Moscow Flyer; and Cheltenham Gold Cup, Kicking King

2006 – Royal & SunAlliance Chase, Star De Mohaison

2007 – Champion Bumper, Cork All Star

2008 – Jewsons Novices' Handicap Chase, Finger Onthe Pulse

2009 – Arkle Challenge Trophy, Forpadydeplasterer

2009 – Champion Hurdle, Punjabi; and Triumph Hurdle, Zaynar;

2010 – Queen Mother Champion Chase, Big Zeb; Coral Cup, Spirit River; and Triumph Hurdle, Soldatino

2011 – Albert Bartlett Novices' Hurdle, Bobs Worth

2012 – Arkle Challenge Trophy, Sprinter Sacre; Neptune Investment Management Novices' Hurdle, Simonsig; RSA Chase, Bobs Worth; Queen Mother Champion Chase, Finian's Rainbow; and Ryanair Chase, Riverside Theatre

2013 – Arkle Challenge Trophy, Simonsig; Queen Mother Champion Chase, Sprinter Sacre; and Cheltenham Gold Cup, Bobs Worth

2014 – Champion Hurdle, Jezki; RSA Chase, O'Faolains Boy; and World Hurdle, More Of That

2015 – Ultima Business Solutions Handicap Chase, The Druids Nephew; and Triumph Hurdle, Peace And Co

2016 – Triumph Hurdle, Ivanovich Gorbatov

THE BEST JOCKEY NEVER TO WIN THE CHAMPIONSHIP – ADRIAN MAGUIRE

Jockeys dream, of course, but to achieve a winner on a first visit to the Cheltenham Festival, as an amateur; and then, the next year, win nothing less than the ultimate steeplechasing prize, the Cheltenham Gold Cup in your first season as a professional rider? That is more than the stuff of dreams.

Irish jockey Adrian Maguire got off to just such an unbelievable start at the Cheltenham Festival, winning the Fulke Walwyn/Kim Muir Chase on Omerta in 1991, off a weight of nine stone 13lbs. He was just short of his twentieth birthday. Then, three weeks after Cheltenham, the pair won the Irish Grand National by a short head over Cahervillahow, carrying ten stone 6lbs. The very next year, he rode the winner of the Gold Cup, Cool Ground. Trainer Toby Balding was aiming the chestnut at the Grand National, but let him take his chances in the Gold Cup as a warm up. In a three-way photo finish, Cool Ground just prevailed from The Fellow and Docklands Express; Toby Balding attributed the success to the forceful riding of his young jockey.

In 1994, riding for Martin Pipe, Adrian Maguire showed that strength again, getting Viking Flagship home by a neck from Travado in that year's Queen Mother Champion Chase.

In later years, however, the Festival eluded Adrian Maguire. He missed it four times in eight years, three of them in succession – once when his mother died unexpectedly, and the remainder due to injury.

Some say it was his daredevil style that caught up with him, and many say he was the best never to win the jockeys' championship, even though one year he scored an amazing 194 victories. The trouble was, Richard Dunwoody rode three more, in one of the most exciting seasonal climaxes.

Adrian is one of the select band of jockeys to have ridden 1,000 winners, but injury forced him to retire in 2002.

Hailing from Kilmessan in County Meath, he now trains in County Cork, homeland of his wife, Sabrina. Sadly, at the time of writing, he looks like joining the growing band of good small Irish trainers to be forced to give up. Racing was his destiny from an early age, as he notched up 200 pony-racing wins and then won the Irish point-to-point championship, during three years that he rode for County Limerick-based Michael Hourigan. He moved to Toby Balding, near Andover in Hampshire, and quickly became champion conditional jockey. The next conditional jockey at Toby Balding's was none other than Tony McCoy.

Toby Balding, who trained winners of the Gold Cup, the Champion Hurdle twice and the Grand National twice, died in 2014, aged seventy-eight.

Adrian Maguire, always generous and well-liked, may be best remembered for sourcing the mighty Denman, producing him to win at the Duhallow point-to-point at Liscarroll, County Cork, in March 2005. Bred by Colman O'Flynn and sold after that first win to be trained in England by Paul Nichols, Denman won his next three races in England, was beaten in the Royal and Sun Alliance novice hurdle at the 2006 Festival, and then won his next nine races consecutively – these included the 2007 Royal and Sun Alliance Chase and the 2008 Cheltenham Gold Cup, beating his stable companion Kauto Star. Denman also finished second in the Gold Cup in the next three years, and is now in honourable retirement.

FIRST LADIES OF CHELTENHAM

It is the Cheltenham Foxhunters, known as the amateurs' Gold Cup. The race is at her mercy, the opposition well held. Her head is down; there are no more fences to jump; legs are pumping away. Suddenly the horse jinks left, believing he is to go out on another circuit instead of going straight up the run-in. In a flash, the unfortunate jockey is on the ground; it almost certainly would have been the same for any of the top jocks. One moment, the teenager has only 150 yards to Cheltenham Festival victory; the next she is ignominiously on the ground.

After understandable tears, her about-to-be-achieved ambition shattered, Jane Mangan bounced back. She is a competent rider with a strong work ethic and a deep knowledge and love of racing.

Nina Carberry and Katie Walsh are sisters-in-law, and the queens of Cheltenham. They have both beaten their famous brothers, Paul and Ruby, in Festival hurdle races at long odds. Nina won the 2005 Fred Winter Juvenile Hurdle on Dabiroun, and she has twice won the Cheltenham Foxhunters, riding On The Fringe to victory in 2015 and 2016. But it is her grasp on the Cross-Country Steeplechase that showcases her skill as much as anything. She is its leading rider, with four wins on three different horses since its inception in 2005 (see page 87). Married to Ted Walsh's son, Ted junior, she gave birth to a baby girl in 2017, who the couple have named Rosie.

Her sister-in-law, Katie Walsh, sister of Ruby, is a well-regarded amateur at Willie Mullins' stable, and won both the National Hunt Chase on Poker De Sivola and the County Hurdle on Thousand Stars at the 2010 Festival. She has also finished third in the Aintree Grand National, the highest-placed lady rider to date.

Another Irish girl to add to the list is Lisa O'Neill, attached to Gordon Elliott's yard. She won the Ladies' Derby at the Curragh in 2010, and then one of Ireland's prestigious staying steeplechases, the 2016 Kerry National in Listowel. She scored on Wrath Of Titans for Gigginstown House Stud off the featherweight of nine stone 3lbs, beating Ireland's top professional men in the process.

But she topped that by landing the JT McNamara four-mile National Hunt Chase on Tiger Roll at the 2017 Cheltenham Festival. Memorably, all three amateur races at the 2017 Festival were won by female riders (Gina Andrews and Bryony Frost for England being the other two).

Gordon Elliott is quick to praise not only Lisa O'Neill's riding, but also her work ethic, an acknowledged prerequisite in his yard – and in Lisa's case, in his office, too, where she helps out three afternoons a week.

Patrick Mullins is quickly closing in on 450 career winners as he chases Ted Walsh's record tally of 545. He lost out on the 2017 Irish amateur championship by one, to Jamie Codd, who took the title for the first time. Going into Punchestown at the close of the season, Jamie was five wins clear. Patrick then rode a memorable treble on the penultimate day, and one more on the last day.

Notably, two of the three wins were Grade 1, which brought his father's prize money won ahead of long-time leader and challenger for the title, Gordon Elliott. It gave Willie Mullins a tenth Irish trainer's championship – by a short head.

Patrick's first Cheltenham Festival win was on Cousin Vinny, in the 2008 Bumper. He won the 2012 Bumper on Champagne Fever, and the 2013 NH Chase on Back In Focus.

A CHELTENHAM CHAMPION – CHARLIE SWAN

Charlie Swan was Irish champion jockey nine times consecutively between 1989–90 and 1997–8. He was twice leading jockey at Cheltenham, in 1993 and 1994. His big-race wins include the Stayers' Hurdle with Trapper John in 1990 and Shuil Ar Aghaidh in 1993; followed by the Royal & Sun Alliance Hurdle the next year, with one of Ireland's most popular horses, Danoli; and the Queen Mother Champion Chase, with Viking Flagship in 1995.

His name will always be best remembered for his association with Istabraq, who won at the Festival for four years in succession. Charlie himself continued riding at least one winner each year at the Festival up to and including his last one in 2002, when he scored on both Scolardy in the Triumph Hurdle, and in the Supreme Novices' Hurdle on the lovely big mare Like-A-Butterfly. He then concentrated solely on training, until 2015, when waning fortune forced him to pack up, another loss to the industry.

POWER SURGE – ROBBIE POWER

To those who saw the damage to his eye after a fall in the 2016 Galway Festival, Robbie Power's career looked as though it might well be over. He was kicked along the turf by another of the twenty runners, resulting in a complex fracture of his left eye-socket, damage to the muscle on the floor of his eye-bed and a broken cheekbone. The injury left him with double vision, and it was only through the use of specially adapted ophthalmic goggles that he was able to return to race-riding some three months later – and with golden results.

One of Robbie Power's many qualities has been loyalty. It was for Jessie Harrington that Robbie won his first race, on a horse owned by his mother called Younevertoldme, at Punchestown in December 2001. In March and April 2017, he rode both the Cheltenham Gold Cup and Irish Grand National winners for Jessie Harrington.

In between, he had been champion conditional jockey in 2003–04; won the Galway Plate for Paddy Mullins on Nearly A Moose in 2003; and in 2007, won the Aintree Grand National on Silver Birch. He had to wait until 2011 for his first Cheltenham Festival winner. This was Bostons Angel in the RSA Chase, trained by Jessica Harrington.

It was never a surprise that Meath man Robbie 'Puppy' Power (so named by friend and neighbour Paul Carberry) would be a natural and gifted horseman. His father, Captain Con Power, showjumped for Ireland in the heady 1970s, when Ireland won the Aga Khan cup several times. His mother Mags competed at Badminton, and Robbie himself won a Young Riders' European Championships Silver Medal. While he turned his hand to racing, his sister Elizabeth became a top Irish eventer. Occasionally, when one of Jessie's horses needs a change of scene, he will take it hunting.

What a magic spring it turned out to be in 2017. Beginning by taking the sport's blue riband, the Cheltenham Gold Cup, on Sizing John (see page 228), Robbie Power was then promptly appointed retained jockey for the horse's owners, Alan and Ann Potts. The effect was almost immediate. At Aintree, Robbie Power rode three winners to become the meeting's leading jockey.

Robbie remains number one to Jessica Harrington, and hot on the heels of Aintree, he won Ireland's biggest NH handicap, the Irish Grand National, on Our Duke, trained by her.

In a pulsating Irish Gold Cup at Punchestown, he won on Sizing John over Djackadam and the gallant Coneygree, who was making a courageous comeback after injury.

HE NEARLY PACKED HIS BAGS – NOEL FEHILY

The fall looked easy enough, almost run-of-the-mill, with the rider coming down most of the way with his horse and then being thrown clear into Warwick's rain-softened turf. But then the horse kept rolling – right over the jockey. The horse got up okay, but the stricken rider lay on the ground, motionless. An ambulance crew was quickly in attendance, and the ground staff prepared to doll off the fence, to prevent the remaining runners from jumping it next time round. Then the jockey got to his feet. He was holding a shoulder and his face was streaked with blood, but he walked off the track and to the ambulance.

Just three days later, Cork-born Noel Fehily was back in the saddle, with three rides booked at Exeter, the last of which he won. Such is a jump jockey's life. Earlier that January 2017 afternoon at Warwick, Noel had ridden two winners. His fall was at the second fence in the feature three-miles five-furlongs BetFred Classic Chase, and he was riding the experienced Kaki De La Pree, trained by Tom Symonds. The fall also hampered the eventual winner, the Irish-bred One For Arthur, whose next outing was to win the Aintree Grand National, no less, partnered by his regular jockey Derek Fox, who hails from County Sligo.

Noel Fehily is now among the senior riders in England, regularly scoring 100 winners in a season, and with a Champion Hurdle and two King Georges under his belt. But his was not an overnight success story. Shortly after he first arrived in England, he nearly packed his bags to return to Ireland. It was autumn, NH racing was not yet in full swing, and he found the scene a bit quiet after the buzz of Irish point-to-points, where he was a sought-after amateur rider.

Horses had not been part of his home life, growing up on a farm near Macroom and Mallow in County Cork, but he took lessons at the local riding school, and progressed to the Cork and Kerry pony-racing circuit from there. He started riding point-to-pointers, and found he loved it, so when he left school at eighteen, he worked for a couple of point-to-point yards.

He was in his early twenties when he arrived at Charlie Mann's yard in Lambourn, still as an amateur. Finding life a bit too quiet, he vowed to return to Ireland if he did not ride five winners by Christmas. He rode six, and, with no regrets and to the good fortune of British racing, he stayed.

Noel's first winner was in a maiden chase at Plumpton, at odds of 16-1 on a horse called Ivy Boy. Shortly after, he rode the horse again at Newbury; there was a short-priced favourite in the field ridden by Richard Dunwoody, but Ivy Boy again won easily. Naturally, Noel was keenly anticipating riding him in the prestigious four-mile National Hunt Chase for amateur riders at the Cheltenham Festival. He could hardly believe his luck in having a horse to ride there in his first season. But a whip offence at Fontwell saw him suspended and forced to watch from the sidelines.

'I was gutted, big time,' he admits – but it taught him a lesson.

'It's so easy to go a couple of smacks over [the limit allowed], but the whips are so soft now that they don't mark the horses. But I feel the rule is for the good, and jockeys ride better for it.'

It was to be another nine years, in 2008, before Noel broke his Festival duck, but it was not as expected.

'I had high hopes for a number, and thought I would get one at last, but none of my fancied mounts did any good.'

He had one ride left, a 50-1 outsider called Silver Jaro in the last race of the Festival, the Vincent O'Brien County Handicap Hurdle, for fellow countryman Tom Hogan. Another Irishman, the canny trainer Tony Martin, had the hotpot called Psycho. It had been backed into short-priced favouritism, and was ridden by the master of riding a waiting race, Paul Carberry. But it was Silver Jaro who prevailed up the infamous Cheltenham hill.

Following this, patience was again required, as Noel sat out both the 2010 and 2011 Festivals through injury.

His moment of glory came in the 2012 Champion Hurdle, on board the Irish-bred Rock On Ruby. And then 2017 capped everything that had gone before, as Noel rode to victory in both the Champion Hurdle and the Queen Mother Champion Chase, described in the last chapter.

FROM TELLY TO REALITY – ANDREW LYNCH

The son of jockey Sean Lynch, Andrew Lynch dreamed as a schoolboy of riding at Cheltenham. The County Meath man says, 'I would rush home early from school and put the telly on when Cheltenham was on. To get the opportunity to ride there is incredible, and to win unbelievable.'

He rode in a point-to-point at Castletown Geoghan, County Westmeath, at the age of sixteen, and finished third. Since then, he has become a regular rider for Henry de Bromhead, and for friend and neighbour Robbie Hennessy.

Andrew's dream of riding a winner at the Cheltenham Festival came true courtesy of Sizing Europe. In that horse's stellar career, Andrew was on board him twenty-six times, winning fifteen. The horse went into the 2010 Arkle with three out of three novice chases and a beginners' chase (for jockey Denis O'Regan) under his belt. It was Andrew's third time at the Festival. His two brothers came over, and they all stayed in a hotel nearby.

Sizing Europe galloped to victory, and as Andrew Lynch rode into the winner's enclosure, he was glad he had his family members there. He also won the cross-country race with Sizing Australia, a race which calls for a different type of skill in a jockey.

The following year, 2011, he rode two winners again, including one of the big three, when he won the Queen Mother with Sizing Europe and the Alfred Bartlett three-mile hurdle on Bertie's Dream for trainer Paul John Gilligan.

'He's been a good supporter for me,' says Andrew.

FAITH REWARDED – PAUL TOWNEND

Most of Hurricane Fly's routine ridden work was undertaken by Paul Townend, and the vast majority of that was done on his own. Otherwise, the danger was that he would 'leave his race on the gallops', so tough and competitive was he alongside other horses.

'The Fly' helped put Paul Townend on the map. He won his first Grade 1 on him in the Royal Bond at Fairyhouse in 2008, when Ruby Walsh was sidelined. Paul rode him eight times and won six Grade Ones, with Ruby Walsh being on board for all his other victories.

From Middleton in County Cork, where his father Tim Townend trained a few point-to-pointers, Paul is also a cousin of now-retired jockey Davy Condon and nephew of jockey Bob Townend. He took the familiar pony-racing route into racing, joining Willie Mullins aged just fifteen as a flat-race apprentice. Since then, Willie's faith in the young rider has been well rewarded – and in the 2010–11 season, he deservedly won the Irish NH jockeys' championship.

Incredibly, four times, Paul has won four races in a day at a race meeting. Of his six Cheltenham Festival winners, his double on the last day in 2017 must be particularly sweet, with the County Hurdle on Arctic Fire, and the Albert Bartlett Novices' Hurdle on Penhill, both for his boss Willie Mullins.

A PLACE WHERE DREAMS ARE MADE – GAVIN SHEEHAN

Thursday, 12 March 2015, Ladbrokes World Hurdle (Grade 1):

'Made all … stayed on strongly.'

The bare form report cannot tell the whole story. A first Grade 1 win for the jockey, a first Cheltenham Festival win, and one of the Big Four at that, for both jockey and trainer. At odds of 14-1.

Gavin Sheehan had dreamt of this moment. He had confidence in his mount Cole Harden for his boss Warren Greatrex, and had predicted their win at a Cheltenham preview evening in Newbury. But the nearer the day got, the more fearful he felt. What if he did something wrong? Or the rain came and turned the going soft? Or things in the race were to go badly? It can happen.

It was after Cole Harden had won the Grade 2 Bet 365 Hurdle at Wetherby that trainer and jockey began to plot the plan, to dream the dream. There was no longer a Big Bucks or the other established staying hurdlers in the World Hurdle field. Maybe it could be their turn. They set about making it a reality.

And now the day had come. Gavin's mother Geraldine, and brother Keith, arrived from Dunmanway in West Cork for their first visit to Cheltenham. Gavin met them there early and the two brothers walked the course together. None of Gavin's family had any previous interest in horses, let alone racing, but this was different.

In the weighing room, he changed into the dark-green-and-orange colours of owners Jill and Robin Eynon. Then former champion conditional jockey Gavin Sheehan sat quietly, alongside more experienced big-race jockeys: English stars Sam Twiston Davies and Daryl Jacob; and his fellow countrymen – Davy Condon, his hero Noel Fehily, superstar Ruby Walsh, the inimitable Paul Carberry, the veteran Davy Russell, and Irish legends Barry Geraghty and AP McCoy. Sam Twiston Davies' mount Saphir Du Rheu, who had beaten Cole Harden the last time they met, was the 5-1 favourite.

Gavin's previous rides that week had proved disappointing. They included a fall in the curtain-raiser, the Supreme Novices' Hurdle, sponsored by Sky Bet, and won by Willie Mullins' Douvan (Ruby Walsh). Gavin was riding Seedling, on whom he had previously notched a treble (and who suffered a fatal fall next time out). The next day, he was tailed-off with Warrantor. It just wasn't happening for him.

Now it was out to the paddock and nervous-looking owners and trainer. Gavin touched his cap in greeting, smiled and made chirpy small talk, his dark-brown eyes taking everything in. Perched on his cap was the Channel 4 head camera. Warren Greatrex gave him the leg-up and reassured him.

'We're the best, you can do it.' And then, crucially, 'I believe in you.' With those words ringing in his ears, Gavin joined the parade and cantered down to the start. Cole Harden was bouncing underneath him; the whole place was electric. They were off, and Gavin got just the start he needed – out in front. The Irish-bred six-year-old by Westerner was a confirmed front-runner, who stayed well. Gavin rode the race as a man with a wise head, allowing his partner to get a breather at halfway and then kicking on for home, Cole Harden grabbing hold of the bit once more.

He 'winged' the second-last and Gavin, feeling 'a lot of horse' beneath him, allowed himself the thought, 'The others still haven't come to me.' He flew the last flight, heard none of the crowd's roars but only his own vocal encouragement to his willing mount, saw the winning line out of the corner of his eye and thought, 'Yes.'

The pair passed the line three-and-a-quarter lengths in front of the favourite, having never seen another horse throughout the race. The placed jockeys, Sam Twiston Davies and Noel Fehily, in turn put their arms around him and patted him on the back, as did a number of the others – it's a close-knit world in the jockeys' ranks. As Gavin turned to walk back, the victory began to sink in. And there, on the rails, were his mother and brother. And on he walked, through the crowds, to the hallowed winners' enclosure.

Barely a dozen years had gone by since the young west Cork rider had asked Santa for a rocking horse. Come Christmas morning, his parents explained that the box was too large to fit into the chimney; they would have to drive down the lane and look for it.

There, tied up to a wall and tacked up, stood a little black pony, Star. Gavin knew at once that this was his present, and promptly clambered on board. He had never sat on a horse before. His father Seanie, who had also never ridden (bar 'borrowing' the odd stray donkey to transport him to school), suggested *he* ride it first. He promptly fell off going down a steep hill, causing laughter all round the family. Then Gavin was led out on him, and spent most of Christmas Day with him. It was a defining moment.

About a year later, and with Star sold on, the lad bought a donkey foal for €100, naming him Little Rocket. It was a portentous name, for he became a top sprinter in donkey derbies. Until that time, Gavin's main thrill had been in emulating cowboys in TV westerns. He read a book to learn how to break in his donkey, but steering was a problem. This was solved by shaking a plastic bag on his right to make him go left, and vice versa. He rode him every day after school, and got him fitter than the rest. Soon he was winning donkey derbies, thanks to the training he put in himself, but also thanks to the support of various people like the Healys and the Sullivans. Gavin had discovered the thrill of racing and, especially, of winning. His first prize brought him €100, exactly the sum he had paid for Little Rocket. It earned him a tilt at Listowel, 'the Cheltenham of donkey derbies'.

At first, his parents would not allow him to miss school for it, but they eventually relented. Once there, Gavin was in for a shock; many of the other donkeys there were prancing around and 'going mad'. It turned out they were being prodded with pig-stickers and nails to make them go faster. Gavin and Little Rocket won their heat, and were second in the final to an 'oversized donkey that looked like a mule. They told us it was an Italian stallion donkey.' Gavin still won €500 for his second place.

Next came the traditional Irish route of pony racing (very different from the heavily regulated and sanitised English version), on a 12.2 called Gypsy Blaze. Thinking himself a jockey, Gavin rode with his stirrup irons too short, fell off on a bend and broke his wrist. He thought about quitting, but his father encouraged him to try again. Ponies brought him many wins, and then it was on to the fifteen-hands Night Owl for the Castle Racing Syndicate (pony racing in Ireland includes races for horses).

'The syndicate members taught me a great deal, in criticism and praise, and I have them to thank for so much,' says Gavin.

His first winner was Court Mac, and his three years of pony racing included being champion on the beach at Dingle, with five winners there. He began riding out for trainer Gerry Culley, where he schooled over point-to-point fences. In his spare time, he and a friend, Barry O'Donevan, jumped their small ponies both ways over those fences, in spite of the slope being the wrong way when they jumped 'backwards' over them.

'The messing about got me keener and more excited,' he recalls.

After leaving school, it was on to a proper job, with Michael Hourigan. 'He looked after me and got me going the right way.' This included his first point-to-point win, on Old Wigmore.

It was while at Hourigan's that Cheltenham first appeared on Gavin's radar, as he listened to stories of the stable's successes there. It made him long to ride in an amateur race there, or at least to lead up a runner (that is, to prepare and groom it, lead it round the paddock, and care for it after the race). But he was not selected, so he joined the rest of the lads and lasses round the television at the Limerick stables to watch as Adrian Heskin won the cross-country race on A New Story.

'Adrian was a great worker and rider,' Gavin says.

The episode focused Gavin, and he moved on to John Joseph Murphy, where he rode in some professional races, winning a race in Thurles. He bought a saddle of Noel Fehily's, 'because he was my hero, riding the likes of Master Minded, et cetera'. The Fehilys lived ten minutes down the road from his home place, and through them he came to England, initially to Charlie Mann in Lambourn. He is currently with Warren Greatrex, who has Fred Winter's wonderful old stables, Uplands.

From the start, Gavin loved Lambourn. 'I was close to Cheltenham. Every conversation revolved around Cheltenham; I love the buzz of the whole place.'

Rides and wins increased and, in the 2013–14 season, he became champion conditional jockey.

To have notched one of the big four races with his first Cheltenham win is remarkable, and a sign that the young jockey is going places.

'Cheltenham is definitely the place where dreams are made,' he says, noting that it hasn't been long since he was an excited, Ireland-bound watcher of Adrian Heskin winning there. Like any young jockey, he dreams of winning the Grand National – but admits he also aspires to the Queen Mother Champion Chase, because of its speed and class.

The World Hurdle may have been Gavin Sheehan's first Festival win, but, God willing, it will surely not be his last. In July 2017, with his stable growing, Warren Greatrex announced that champion jockey Richard Johnson was to be his first jockey, enabling Gavin Sheehan to 'spread his wings and ride out for other people', while emphasising that there would still be rides for the young man from his stable.

PRE-TRIALS AND TRIBULATIONS

The last Saturday of January is established as pre-Cheltenham trials day on both sides of the Irish Sea. At Cheltenham itself, the day sees the Cotswold Chase, for which in 2017 the hot pot Thistlecrack was expected to extend his unbeaten record over fences and shorten his price for the Gold Cup, which was already odds on. It didn't turn out that way, as we shall see.

A bonus in 2017 was the Clarence House two-mile chase, rerouted from frozen-off Ascot the previous week, and the thrilling prospect of Un De Sceaux. During the day, both he and the JCB juvenile trial winner, Defi Du Seuil, went on to score at the Festival.

Over in Leopardstown, a similar card is held, the feature of which is the Arkle Chase. This was won by Some Plan, whose three rivals all fell or unseated – so not too much Cheltenham forecast was achieved.

By this time, some of the big hopes for the 2017 Cheltenham Festival had already fallen by the wayside. In Ireland, the news that Annie Power was out of the Festival was a huge blow, especially as Willie Mullins had lost the hugely talented Vautour in November. In his sixteen-race career, Vautour was only out of the first two once, when he fell in the Melling Chase at Aintree, and he loved Cheltenham, where he was unbeaten at the Festival.

Vautour won the Supreme Novices' Hurdle at the 2014 Festival, the JLT (Golden Miller) Novices' Chase in 2015, and the Ryanair Chase in 2016. He was ante-post second favourite for the 2017 Cheltenham Gold Cup. He was only seven when he died.

For England, Coneygree had also been ruled out of trying to regain the Gold Cup crown he won in 2015.

But back to Cheltenham trials day, and the Cotswold Chase. Odds-on favourite for the Gold Cup is Thistlecrack. Trained by rural Dorset's one-time dairy farmer with a few horses, turned hugely successful trainer with a few dairy cows, Colin Tizzard, naturally Thistlecrack's price here is even shorter. So far, he is unbeaten in three steeplechases – and at the 2016 Festival, he landed the World/Stayers' Hurdle. Lined up against him is a decent field, including 2015 Grand National hero Many Clouds, trained in Lambourn by Oliver Sherwood for owner Trevor Hemmings. He held an engagement for the 2017 Gold Cup, but the main aim was to be the first since Red Rum in the 1970s to regain the Grand National prize. He was already rare in a Grand National victor in resuming winning ways on the racecourse.

At Cheltenham in January 2017, in as fine a steeplechase as one could see, Thistlecrack overtook Many Clouds at the last, but the old hero was not for capitulating and in a pulsating finish he prevailed – only to collapse and die after the winning line. This, thankfully, is an extremely rare occurrence, but all the more devastating when it happens.

Many Clouds, with an English owner and trainer and only one jockey throughout his career, Leighton Aspell, was Irish-bred through and through.

By Cloudings out of Bobbing Back, by Bob Back, he was bred by Aidan Aherne in Middleton, County Cork. Bobbing Back ran just three times in her life, and was never placed, yet she produced a Grand National winner who was as game as they come. Some people spend squillions trying to breed such a horse

CHAPTER 8

CHELTENHAM
FESTIVAL 2017

TUESDAY, 14 MARCH 2017

ATTENDANCE: 66,019

The station is heaving, the train already almost full, as it draws in for more passengers to squeeze on. Most hold a racing paper, wear a badge for the races, and either scan for tips or chat with their mates about the day ahead. Many of them are already drinking beer.

It might have been hard to get on, but it is even more difficult to get off. Cheltenham Spa station is a seething throng of race-goers. It has many extra staff directing the masses to the buses and taxis, and they exhort people to have their tickets ready. Few do, and the queue winds ever more slowly as a result. We snake slowly between the temporary barriers, air-port-terminal style, to the front of a bus line that stretches as far as the eye can see. The town is heaving, too, and the journey is slow, but I chat to the three ladies sitting next to me.

They are from Tralee in County Kerry, and they have been coming every year for ten years. Geraldine Counihan, Sheila Kelly and Joan Barry have been friends since they first started school at the age of four. Joan's late father, Jimmy Barry, was a steward of the Irish National Hunt Committee and chairman of the late, lamented Tralee Racecourse; it was sold in 2008 for building, but then the financial crash happened.

Geraldine says, 'It was devastating for the town.'

She used to come to Cheltenham with her father, and so has been a regular for about twenty-five years. The ladies fly into Birmingham and book into the Ibis Style year on year, and then take the train and shuttle bus to and from the racecourse each day.

'We have small bets,' says Geraldine, 'and we love to see the stars. We watch by the railings on the lawn, so that we can see them close up when they come in.

'We're addicted now, we have the bug.'

It has taken an hour from the train arriving to walking in to the racecourse, but everyone is in good form and the one sure bet of the day is that they will enjoy themselves. We walk from the bus up past the stables and the lines of horseboxes: Alan King, Paul Nicholls, Jonjo O'Neill and a fleet of Irish boxes are all parked together; there are several for Mullins, Shark Hanlon, Gordon Elliott, DT Hughes. Sentimental thoughts of Dessie, there; the late trainer's daughter Sandra went on to hold the licence – but in late April 2017, stunned the racing world by announcing her retirement, as it was no longer financially viable for her. Yet another regrettable loss to the racing world.

Cheltenham racecourse is humming, buzzing, and the parade of old favourites is in progress: Forpadydeplasterer was successful in the Arkle Chase for Kerry trainer Tom Cooper; since retiring he has twice won the

Racehorse to Riding Horse class at the Royal Dublin Show. Rubi Light was placed in the Ryanair Chase for County Meath trainer Robbie Hennessy. Others include Balthazar King, a Cheltenham cross-country specialist and runner-up in the Grand National, who now hunts in Wiltshire with Izzi Beckett, wife of flat trainer Ralph, known as Rafe. Big Bucks is a four-times winner of the Stayers' Hurdle. Former Champion Hurdler Punjabi, Queen Mother Champion Chase-winner Finian's Rainbow, Gold Cup winners Long Run and the mighty Denman parade past, all drawing applause and evoking cherished memories.

A wander through the Guinness Village and one could be in a different world: the concourse is packed solid with groups standing around drinking and laughing, cheerfully oblivious to the rest of Cheltenham, with their different clothing and approach. Most will stay there, placing their bets, watching their horse's progress on the big screen or from the temporary Guinness stand, meeting friends and enjoying themselves.

An Englishwoman visiting the Guinness Village for the first time remarked that never before had she seen the queue for the men's toilets longer than the women's!

In no time, the first race is off, and the traditional roar erupts from 66,000 throats as the tapes rise on the Supreme Novices' Hurdle – and the first of several shock results. The favourite is Melon, trained by Willie Mullins and ridden by Ruby Walsh; they finish second. Willie has four of the fourteen runners. Nicky Henderson has two, and his River Wylde finishes third. Ireland also has one each from Henry de Bromhead, Shark Hanlon and Gordon Elliott, and it is his horse who springs the first surprise, not just for his long price of 25-1, but because in his last three starts Labaik has refused to start. Fearing further embarrassment on the biggest stage, and an almost certain ban for the horse from racing should it happen again, Gordon was not inclined to bring the grey six-year-old. The owners, naturally, were keen to have a runner in Cheltenham, and on the couple of times he had deigned to race properly Labaik had shown real ability, winning twice. However, even the sands of Laytown beach had failed to interest him, and his form, both flat and hurdling, included four RRs (refused to race). Another time, he stood still in the stalls before eventually finishing eighteenth of eighteen; and in his most recent venture he had eventually started long after the others had gone.

It was a brave move to bring him to the biggest jumping stage of all.

Many little things had been tried at home in Cullentra to sweeten him up. Here at Cheltenham, there were other factors – the buzz of the crowd, the jingling atmosphere and, down at the start, the long-held English tradition (not observed in Ireland) of the assistant starter carrying a 'long tom', a hunting whip that, if necessary, he can crack *behind* a recalcitrant horse. A flick of the wrist holding the handle results in the short, thin lash at the end of the long leather thong actually breaking the sound barrier, causing a mini sonic boom. It did not touch the horse, but this was enough to set Labaik off on his historic journey.

Now, having weaved his way through to lead at the last and draw ahead up the famous (or infamous) finishing hill, another factor emerges. His jockey. Riding sensation is not too strong a term. Jack Kennedy is just seventeen years old. He passed his driving test only last month. He is a mature young man, for all his adolescence. By his own admission, he is laid-back, and nothing fazes him. The Kerryman has been riding from four, pony racing from nine, and is now nearing two years in NH racing, based with Gordon Elliott.

The pony racing, in which he rode 241 winners, including the coveted Dingle Derby three times, has given him balance and honed a racing brain. Incredibly, the Supreme Novices' Hurdle is his one-hundredth NH winner, and it is a Grade 1. In the unsaddling enclosure, he is surrounded by his large family, owner Aidan O'Ryan, friends John Boylan and Anthony O'Sullivan and journalists, among others. He maintains a broad smile and answers questions not just patiently, let alone resignedly, but with refreshing openness.

'It's brilliant,' he smiles. 'Everything went smoothly and he [the horse] didn't think of stopping. From twelve or thirteen, I've watched Gordon's horses, and Paul Carberry.'

Jack Kennedy is coolness personified.

'It's a dream come true,' he says. Having broken his leg twice the previous summer, he also already knows the downsides of racing.

'At the time, I thought winning the Dingle Derby was as big as you can get, but this is definitely the best day of my life.'

Labaik reverted to his old ways at Punchestown a month later, but was brought out again later in the week and ran a great race in open company, only to suffer possibly a career-ending injury.

Irish trainers made a record entry of 715 over the four days and twenty-eight races of the 2017 Festival, beating the previous best of 647 in 2015; there were 601 in 2016.

Altior, bred in Ireland by the classy High Chaparral, duly won the Arkle for Nicky Henderson and jockey Nico de Boinville, but not as fluently as many had expected, and nor did he sprint clear on the run-in. It was easy to speculate on what might have been had Charbel not fallen at the second-last when still leading. Nevertheless, Altior's winning record of five from five hurdle races and five from five chases remains intact.

The feature on day one was the Stan James Champion Hurdle, an event JP McManus has won five times previously. His first three were with one of the all-time greats, Istabraq, who enabled JP to take the trophy home from 1998 to 2000. JP then had to wait ten years until his next one, with Binocular in 2010, and four years later it was the turn of Jezki.

His game My Tent Or Yours finished as runner-up in 2014 to JP's Jezki. He missed the 2015 season, and returned to finish runner-up again in 2016, to the mare Annie Power.

Could he make it third time lucky now, or would younger, faster legs prevail? My Tent Or Yours was the old man of the party at ten years old; The New One, another horse who always tries hard, was a year younger. Irish-bred, like My Tent Or Yours, it was his fourth attempt at the Champion Hurdle. The remaining runners ranged in age from five to eight.

JP had two other runners besides Tent – the favourite, Yanworth (trained by Alan King) and Buveur D'Air, trained, like Tent, by Nicky Henderson.

The Irish contingent numbered just three, with two for Willie Mullins and one for Henry de Bromhead, the fancied Petit Mouchoir.

But it was JP's day – not with Yanworth, who finished seventh of the twelve, but Buveur D'Air, whose jockey Noel Fehily said afterwards, 'I couldn't believe how well he was going at the top of the hill. I had to take a pull.'

The ever-game My Tent Or Yours finished second for the third time in the Champion Hurdle. The win brought up fifty winners for JP at Cheltenham, and, as usual, he was quick to praise the team around him. He smiled benignly as he lifted the trophy for the banks of photographers, and his wife Noreen, wearing a fetching baby-pink outfit, smiled proudly.

Nicky Henderson sympathised with Barry Geraghty, JP's retained jockey who is injured, and thanked the team at Seven Barrows, including long-time head lad Albert 'Corky' Browne and groom Hannah Ryan.

'It doesn't just happen,' he noted.

As Hannah led the winner away, smiling broadly, there were more beams on the trophy podium, where Noel Fehily was joined by his two young children, Niamh and Michael, and his wife, Natasha. Remarkably, they were seen to repeat the process ...

Next up was the OLBG Mares' Hurdle, in which Willie Mullins generally has a strong hand. This time he was represented by the favourite, Limini, and Vroum Vroum Mag, both owned by Rich and Susannah Ricci, but Apple's Jade thwarted his pair for Gordon Elliott and Bryan Cooper.

The Gordon Elliott stable took the four-mile JT McNamara novice chase for amateur riders, too, with Lisa O'Neill on Tiger Roll, a horse who, three years earlier, had won the Triumph Hurdle for juveniles over half the distance.

The seven-year-old had been working well at home. Wearing blinkers, he put his best foot forward for Lisa.

She said, 'It's surreal, to be honest. It's an overwhelming feeling.'

Gordon was full of praise. 'She's decent and is an absolute star. I'm delighted for her. I knew after three fences he was on a going day. I can't believe it. To train three winners on the first day of Cheltenham.'

The last race of the day, a handicap chase, also went to Ireland, with the seven-year-old Tully East, trained for owner Barry Connell by Curragh-based trainer Alan Fleming, and skilfully ridden by Denis O'Regan, avoiding fallers. Seven horses came to the last with a chance, but it was Tully East who ran on the best.

Alan Fleming said afterwards, 'Denis is very astute and clever. He is some man for the big day.'

The day finished with four Irish-trained winners, and three from England; so far, so normal. But the biggest surprise of the day was that there had been no Mullins winner.

On the shuttle bus back to the station, widowed brothers Seamus and Micky Kelliher, from Listowel in County Kerry, chat about their day. They have been coming to the Festival for twenty years, just the two of them. They were widowed about thirteen years ago, and have seven daughters between them.

They fly into Bristol and stay in a hotel there, taking the train and shuttle bus to Cheltenham each day.

'We like the whole atmosphere, and to back a few winners – but we've had none today.'

But they'd be back the next day to try again.

WEDNESDAY, 15 MARCH 2017

ATTENDANCE: 57,681

Cunning plan: I take a train an hour later. There are just two carriages, and not quite filled, so it is a much easier exit and the time from station to course is just twenty-five minutes. This allows enough time to see the runners parade for the first race, and, were it wanted, to place a bet.

This was a day of beautiful warm sunshine; of fourth-time-lucky in the big one, the Queen Mother Champion Chase; and of four more wins for Ireland, but, once more, no Mullins winner.

It began with English-trained winners in the first two, with Mite Bite shading his stable companion Whisper by a nose – the width of a hair that would surely be fairer to call a dead heat – after giving away a clear lead by veering across the course towards the exit in the RSA Novices' Steeplechase. Both are trained by Nicky Henderson. The England–Ireland score now stands at 5-4 to the home side.

The Coral Handicap Hurdle brought the scores level, with Supasundae scoring at 16-1 for Jessie Harrington and Robbie Power, and owners Alan and Ann Potts. The win made Jessie Harrington the leading woman trainer at the Cheltenham Festival, bringing her score to nine, having begun with Space Trucker in the Grand Annual eighteen years earlier. Even better was to come for team Jessie and Robbie.

The Coral Cup is a handicap and had twenty-five runners, and the closest any of the four Willie Mullins-trained horses could get was eighth, while the Gordon Elliott-trained favourite Tombstone trailed in last but one.

The sun poured down for the Queen Mother Champion Chase and I went down to the rails on the lawn, by the chute where the runners go out.

This was one to watch, not to bet on. To witness the superiority of Douvan. Or so we thought.

Douvan was unbeaten in his last fourteen races – the first of those in France, and the rest for Willie Mullins. Paul Townend has been on board three times; Patrick Mullins once, when they won the Racing Post Novice Chase at Leopardstown, beating Sizing John for the third of what was to be seven times (five seconds, two thirds); and Ruby Walsh the remaining nine times. His odds of 2-9 reflected the regard in which he is held. Barring accidents (and he is a superb jumper), he was a 'racing certainty'.

Nine others lined up to make a race of it – competing for the minor placings, they believed. Henry de Bromhead was the only other Irish trainer represented, and his Special Tiara has twice before been placed third in this race. The betting suggested the ten-year-old would do no better than that again. Fox Norton and God's Own were both better fancied to place behind Douvan, the highest-rated horse in NH racing.

Special Tiara – 'Mr T' at home – had actually run in the race three times already, coming sixth behind Sire De Grugy in 2014, third beaten three lengths by Dodging Bullets in 2015, and in 2016 third again, behind the mighty Sprinter Sacre. His CV shows him to be one of the most reliable, consistent steeplechasers, but he is often beaten as much by the prevalent deep ground in Ireland as by other horses.

They were off, and Douvan went straight into the lead, but only for one fence. Noel Fehily and Special Tiara took over at the second, and stayed there, jumping slickly, galloping relentlessly. Douvan looked almost novicey at the third and fourth, and uncharacteristically made another mistake three out. Clearly, for whatever reason, he was out of sorts, and faded in the last half-mile.

Special Tiara, meanwhile, just kept galloping, and was two lengths clear at the last. Then, up that long, uphill finish, Fox Norton challenged strongly, closing with every stride. Special Tiara, cajoled by Noel Fehily, dug down to his deepest reserves to hold off the challenge and score one of the most deserved and popular wins.

Riding in on Douvan, unplaced, Ruby looked dejected.

Afterwards, Henry de Bromhead admitted, 'I was waiting for Douvan to come out of the pack. Then it was, "We have a bit of a chance," and then it was, "Will we get home or not?" But the horse was foot-perfect and got into a rhythm; I was hoping for a place. This is incredible.'

'When you have your ground, you have your horse,' Heather de Bromhead pointed out to me.

Noel Fehily said, 'I was very happy with him down the back. I got a breather in for him. I thought Douvan would be stalking, and I was expecting to be challenged.'

Henry added, 'This was his year. It hasn't sunk in yet, but I shall enjoy today.'

There were more happy scenes at the prize-giving with the whole Fehily family again.

'The children will think this winning is easy,' Noel laughed.

Interestingly, Special Tiara was the only English-bred horse in the race, being by Kayf Tara out of a Bob Back mare.

One of Special Tiara's most devoted fans could not be there. Nicole Kent, Henry de Bromhead's secretary, was holding the fort back in Waterford.

Later, back home, Henry posted on his website: 'That was just incredible, but truly no horse deserves it more … I'm delighted for his owner, Sally Rowley-Williams, as she is such an enthusiastic owner and loves her horses so much … Noel gave him the perfect ride.'

How good it was to see Sir AP McCoy at the Festival, looking fuller in the face and so much healthier than in his riding days. Gone was the gaunt, white face, the jutting bones, the lean frame.

He says he's put on two stone since retiring almost two years ago. Well, it suits him. Jockeys really do deprive their bodies to make their racing weights.

At Lambourn's traditional Good Friday open day in 2017, he was competing, as usual, in things like jockeys' show-jumping and mounted gymkhana games. (At least there was no camel racing this time; he won that a couple of years previously.) He and John Francome also gave a masterclass in schooling over hurdles.

But what stood out most was his patience among the huge crowds as child after child, bravely, timidly, only occasionally boldly, approached him for an autograph or, especially, a photograph, for which he invariably put his arm around the youngster. Not a single one was turned down, until organiser Nicky Henderson could be heard bellowing down the PA, 'Would AP *please* come to the ring and get his pony for the mounted games. We're waiting.'

Ireland, and Ulster in particular, are rightly proud of their famous son.

The day ends with still not one winner for Willie Mullins. Rumours are rife: of the virus, or that he's lost his touch, or that the loss of those sixty horses is showing. Willie maintains his composure, smiling like the gentleman he is. Douvan has gone off to a veterinary centre to be scanned; the next day, a hair stress fracture of the pelvis is diagnosed.

Most trainers and riders would be pleased with one Festival winner, but Willie Mullins is not most trainers; he has been leading trainer for five of the last six years.

The measure of the man is that Willie was treating defeat the same as all his victories, just as Rudyard Kipling would wish:

… If you can meet with Triumph and Disaster

And treat those two impostors just the same …

THURSDAY, 16 MARCH 2017
ATTENDANCE: 66,200

At the last minute, I decide not to take the train, but to watch the television coverage at home.

What a difference a day makes. Or, as Brough Scott exclaimed to television viewers, 'Today was the wow factor.'

From the start, it became a Mullins/Walsh benefit. Yorkhill, owned by Andrea and Graham Wylie, won the opening JLT Novices' Chase. It was a masterly Ruby Walsh ride, holding the horse up all the way although he was pulling. The horse was clever, too, because he twice had to side-step fallers. The combination then faced a wall of three horses, but Ruby managed to steer Yorkhill through on the inside to the last fence. Yorkhill then made a jumping mistake, causing him to nod his head on landing, but they survived that error and stormed up the hill to beat Top Notch by a length. It was Yorkhill's ninth win under Rules from just ten runs, but he has his quirky side.

Ruby said afterwards, 'He's a racehorse. To me, he has Gold Cup written all over him. He might have a kink in him, but he has a massive engine.'

Of his blank two days, Ruby said, 'Everything can't go right all the time. It's sport; you keep looking forward to the next race.'

Willie said, 'Yorkhill's not an easy ride. If he [Ruby] let him pass one horse, he'd be in the lead at the next.'

His owner, Graham Wylie, told viewers, 'He jumped really well, and he had to be clever as well. If he settles, he could stay.'

Evidently, he is not an easy horse to deal with at home, but his form record is excellent, and Ruby's words should never be dismissed. The cheer that greeted them into the winners' enclosure spoke volumes for the esteem in which these connections are held, and the relief at their ending their blank two days.

It was the turn of a small Irish stable next, and such a tonic to see that it can be done. Patrick Kelly is a David among the Goliaths. He houses just five horses in his Athenry, County Galway, yard, but one of them, Presenting Percy, was good enough to win the Pertemps Network Final hurdle, in the hands of one of Ireland's most experienced jockeys, Davy Russell. Amazingly, trainer and rider won this race for the second year in succession, having won it in 2016 with Mall Dini, owned, like Presenting Percy, by Philip Reynolds, son of Ireland's former Taoiseach (Prime Minister) Albert Reynolds. So Patrick Kelly had a 100% record of two winners from two runners in the last two years.

After the race, Pat Kelly said, 'He is a horse going places, and I am looking forward to him going chasing next year.'

He added, 'Davy Russell was brilliant.'

Owner Philip Reynolds said, 'Last year was a dream come true. Davy is unbelievable round here, a master.'

Just over two decades earlier, Pat Kelly had had less luck with the only other two runners he has ever had in Cheltenham. The first, in 1990, fell and broke its leg. Four years later, his sole runner unseated his amateur rider – a certain Willie Mullins. The long gap between Festival runners ensued, but patience was doubly rewarded at the 2016 and 2017 Festivals.

* * *

Since the Festival was extended to four days in 2005, it has featured twin top races on the Thursday – the Ryanair Chase over two miles five furlongs, and the three-mile Stayers' Hurdle, both Grade 1 and both, in 2017, with an equal prize pot to the winner of £170,850.

This time we were to witness, to many viewers' eyes, the outstanding performance of the meeting, in the Ryanair Chase. Ruby Walsh started off by trying to keep Un De Sceaux tucked in at the rear. Un De Sceaux, owned by Edward O'Connell, was having none of it, and by the fourth fence, he had pulled and jumped his way to the front, literally running away. The pair never saw another horse, and at one stage were five lengths clear, with some of Un De Sceaux's jumping being out of this world, flamboyant, enthusiastic and accurate. By two out, only a fall could prevent him from winning, and he never looked in any danger.

Willie Mullins said afterwards, 'He's everything you'd want in a racehorse: brave, strong and sound. He's an iron horse.'

Ruby Walsh said, 'I kind of knew he'd run away with me at some stage. He jumped super; I was only keeping a leg either side of him.'

It had been a scintillating exhibition round, from a truly exciting horse.

Runner up, at a respectful one-and-a-half lengths, was Gigginstown House Stud's Sub Lieutenant, giving Michael O'Leary his fifth second placing in ten years of sponsoring the race.

Next up was the joint feature, the Sunbet Stayers' Hurdle. It was Mullins and Walsh again, this time with Nichols Canyon. Hot favourite, and to many people's eyes banker of the meeting after Douvan, was Unowhatimeanharry, but he could only finish third. Dividing them was the 33-1 chance Lil Rockerfeller, with the ever-game Cole Harden, who tried hard to make all, in fourth.

The best picture of the day was of Katie Walsh greeting her brother with unbounded joy as they pulled up. She finished sixth on Clondaw Warrior at 33-1, one of three Mullins runners.

The biggest disappointment was former Champion Hurdler Jezki, who only had one finisher behind him. His trainer, Jessie Harrington, from Moone in County Kildare, was soon to find compensation.

So that was three, so far, for Walsh and Mullins on day three. After their bare two days, Ruby Walsh was about to achieve a new record: riding four winners in one day at the Festival, all of them for Willie Mullins. The pair had so nearly achieved this in 2015, only to be denied by the totally unexpected fall of Annie Power at the last flight in the Mares' Hurdle.

This time, there was no such disaster, and his win in the Trull House Mares' Hurdle was with the 11-8 favourite, the appropriately named Let's Dance. Ruby Walsh produced her brilliantly at the last flight. Leading her in, her lass Polly said, 'I love this filly so much.'

Owner Rich Ricci – whose odds-on Douvan had been beaten the day before, whose stars Annie Power and Faugheen were absent through injury, and whose Vautour had been killed at home in the autumn – said, 'It's such a relief to get one … it's been a brutal season, but there's no future in history. You've got to keep looking forward.

'This game would tame a lion, it's up and down.'

When Noel Meade was told that this was his first chase winner at the Festival, after Road To Respect won Thursday's handicap chase, he said, 'I wasn't aware we hadn't had a chase winner at the Festival, but I suppose we haven't had too many runners. Harbour Pilot was third in two Gold Cups, and Road To Riches has gone close – but at least we've ended that run.'

Noel Meade is a much-respected former champion trainer. His first Festival winner, back in 2000, was Sausalito Bay in the Supreme Novices' Hurdle. And the horse he beat? Best Mate, future triple Gold Cup winner.

Owner Michael O'Leary said Bryan Cooper gave the chestnut Road To Respect a 'peach of a ride' after the horse screwed badly over the first fence. Cooper demonstrated his ability by staying in the saddle.

A tweet from Robbie McNamara was made public that evening. It read: 'Yesterday Willie Mullins' yard had a "virus" and his gallops needed to be changed. Glad to see they got it sorted so quick.'

FRIDAY, 17 MARCH 2017
ATTENDANCE: 70,160

Saint Patrick's Day. Gold Cup day.

Incredibly, Willie Mullins has had the runner-up *six* times in the Gold Cup, but has never won it. Can that change today?

First up was the JCB Triumph Hurdle for four-year-olds, and it went England's way via the prolific winner Defi Du Seuil, trained by Philip Hobbs and ridden by Richard Johnson. The owner is Ireland's JP McManus, and this win makes it six in a row for the impressive young horse.

By contrast, it was a case of turning the clock back in the next. Former Champion Hurdle runner-up Arctic Fire defied both top weight and an absence of 418 days to score for Willie Mullins and jockey Paul Townend, at 20-1 in the Randox Health County Handicap Hurdle. At one point, it looked as though there might have been an even bigger Irish shock when Wakea, trained by Karl Thornton, was giving 3lb-claiming jockey Donagh Meyler the thrill of a lifetime, some twenty-five lengths clear of the remaining twenty-four runners.

The winner gave an outstanding display to win after such a long lay-off. The feat was fully appreciated by owner Nick Peacock, under his Wicklow Bloodstock banner.

'Paul has been very lucky for me, and I'm a big fan,' he said of the jockey. 'He's very tender.'

Paul Townend made it a quick long-priced double in the three-mile Grade 1 Albert Bartlett Novices' Hurdle, riding a superb waiting race on Penhill for Willie Mullins and owner Tony Bloom, coming from almost last to first. Monalee tried his heart out for jockey David Mullins, but could not match the winner; she is trained by Henry de Bromhead and owned by Barry Maloney.

* * *

So now it is time for the big one, not just of today, but of the whole meeting. Festival Fever is at its height, as more than 70,000 people pour into Prestbury Park to witness first-hand National Hunt racing's premier event, the Cheltenham Gold Cup, sponsored by Timico.

Willie Mullins was represented by Djakadam, runner-up in both the previous two years, and he considered that the eight-year-old, owned by the Riccis, was more mature and spot-on ready for the race. In the absence of ante-post favourite Thistlecrack, he was favourite, closely followed by Native River and the popular veteran Cue Card.

Thirteen lined up to face the starter at 3.30pm on St Patrick's Day. Four of them were from Ireland: Sizing John (Jessie Harrington), Champagne West (Henry de Bromhead) and Outlander (Gordon Elliott) in addition to Djakadam. Jonjo O'Neill had previous Stayers' Hurdle winner More Of That and Minella Rocco. Seven of the jockeys were Irish.

Adding interest was the fact that Lizzie Kelly was only the second female to ride in the race. Her mount, Tea For Two, had finished close up in the King George. It was also on this horse that she had become the first female rider in England to win a Grade 1.

They were off, and Tea For Two made a monumental and uncharacteristic blunder at the second fence, giving his rider no chance of staying in the saddle. Up front Native River, who had vied for favouritism, looked to be enjoying himself at a good gallop. Champagne West and the baby of the field, six-year-old Bristol De Mai, were up with the leader. Those watching closely spotted Sizing John jumping like a slick veteran on the inside in mid-division, gaining ground at each fence.

On the crucial final downhill stretch three out, before the sweep in on the final circuit, Djakadam joined Native River at the head of affairs. Here, Cue Card fell for the second year in succession, but this time he hadn't looked like winning; luckily, both he and Paddy Brennan were unscathed.

At the second-last, Djakadam made an uncharacteristic mistake, and Sizing John jumped into the lead, extending his advantage to three lengths at the last fence. He flew this impressively, and swept to a decisive victory under jockey Robbie Power.

Meanwhile, a hard-fought tussle took place for the minor honours, with Minella Rocco gaining second in the final stride by a short head from the brave Native River, and Djakadam only half a length back in fourth.

Cheers greeted Sizing John into the winners' enclosure. Surprisingly, this was the first Festival at which jockey Robbie Power had won, though he had won the Grand National ten years previously on Silver Birch. He had recently had back trouble and eye problems, so these victories were extra special.

Also surprising was that it was Jessie Harrington's first runner in the race. In the post-race press conference, she quipped, 'I have not had a horse I have considered for the Gold Cup before – they have either been two-milers, handicappers or not good enough.'

One could not help but think of Henry de Bromhead, who had found the horse, nurtured him and trained him to four successes, including in the Grade 1 Future Champions Novices' Hurdle at the Leopardstown Christmas Festival.

Jessie Harrington, for her part, was gracious in her acknowledgement of the role he had played.

She said, 'I do feel very sorry for Henry de Bromhead, with this horse and Supasundae. He did all the hard work; I have only inherited them.

'I only got them in September, I had to get to know them, how to train them. Henry had done all the work, and he bought them.

Douvan had been Sizing John's nemesis. He was placed behind him no less than seven times, including on his first outing for Jessie.

After that, he was stepped up to two-and-a-half miles. Having been successful over that distance, jockey Robbie Power suggested trying three miles in the Irish Gold Cup at Leopardstown in February, which he won.

How ironic that, in avoiding the 'certainty' of Douvan in the Queen Mother, Un De Sceaux had opted for the Ryanair Chase, to put up the most exciting performance of the meeting, and Sizing John had been stepped up to the Gold Cup. Either of them could have won the Queen Mother, if only one of them had opted for it – but then Special Tiara would not have gained his much-deserved win for Henry de Bromhead.

Robbie Power said that because Sizing John had been mainly two-mile-chasing, he was fast over the fences, and he was able to give him a breather when he wanted to. 'The race couldn't have really gone better,' he said, although he had not originally intended to take the inside route.

'But riding for Jessie is fantastic. She never ties you down to instructions; you can use your brain and go where there is a bit of room. It was Plan B to go down the inside; I found myself there and got a great run round.

'It's unbelievable – I was only twenty-five when I won the National, and I thought I was going to win everything in racing. When you're thirty-five, you're not so confident! You appreciate it a bit more, and this is something that will stay with me forever.'

A naturally delighted Jessie Harrington, who had turned seventy in February, added, 'It is the jewel in the crown. As long as I've been watching racing, it's a race I'd dreamed of winning, so to do it is special. It has not really sunk in yet. I can't believe it's true.'

She became the first Irish trainer to win the big three Festival races – the Queen Mother Champion Chase twice with Moscow Flyer, the Champion Hurdle with Jezki, and now the Gold Cup with Sizing John. Only Fred Rimell, Fred Winter, Nicky Henderson and Paul Nicholls have achieved that before.

For the record, Lizzie Kelly, who must have Irish connections with a name like that, achieved glorious vindication three weeks later, winning the Grade 1 Betfair Bowl at Aintree and beating no less than Cue Card. Tea For Two had been popping away, and was beautifully ridden to come to the front when it mattered. The pair had been just three-and-a-half lengths behind Thistlecrack in the King George, and were beaten a head and a short head in a three-way fight for second place, so his place in the Gold Cup was justified, and his Aintree win was sweet redemption.

Jessie Harrington's Gold Cup day was not yet over. Her sixth runner and third winner of the Festival – and Robbie Power's third win – was to come in the Festival's final race, the Johnny Henderson Grand Annual Steeplechase. This was the 10-1 shot Rock The World, owned by Michael Buckley, who had finished third in the same race the previous year.

The Johnny Henderson Grand Annual Handicap Chase brings down the curtain on the 2017 Festival. Ireland is already home and hosed for the Prestbury Cup between England and Ireland, with eighteen Irish wins to nine trained in the UK.

For Jessie to cap the final day of the 2017 Festival with a third winner was all the more special, because the Grand Annual is named after Johnny Henderson, father of her great friend and fellow trainer Nicky. His home at Seven Barrows, Lambourn, is traditionally her base for Cheltenham, and every year he stays with her for the Punchestown Festival a month later.

Jessie said, 'I had one winner in 2011, and it has been six dry years since then. To take home three this year, including the Gold Cup, is unbelievable. It's fantastic for Robbie as well.

'What a day! Rock The World loves quick ground and is a beautiful jumper. He absolutely pinged the last, and didn't stop all the way up the hill.'

In a rare interview with JP McManus in the paddock after his third winner of the meeting, with Defi Du Seuil in the JCB Triumph Hurdle, he naturally said how pleased he was with his horses. Winning the Champion Hurdle with Buveur D'Air brought him 'great joy'. It was also his fiftieth Festival winner, his first being Mister Donovan in the Sun Alliance Novices' Hurdle on St Patrick's Day 1982.

But JP received the biggest round of applause when he praised all the staff who look after the horses, paying tribute to their dedication and hard work.

Absent from action through injury – and much missed – were Barry Geraghty (six broken ribs); Coneygree and Don Cossack (Cheltenham Gold Cups in 2015 and 2016); Thistlecrack (2016 Stayers' Champion and antepost favourite for the 2017 Gold Cup); Faugheen and Annie Power (the previous two Champion Hurdle winners).

The final roll of honour saw Gordon Elliott take home his first trainer's title. He and Willie Mullins ended with six winners apiece, but the title went to Gordon because he scored three seconds to Willie's two. Gordon also gained three thirds, while Willie had four. In third place, Nicky Henderson had three winners, six seconds and four thirds, which left Jessie Harrington in fourth, with a straight three wins. Henry de Bromhead was fifth, with one win, two seconds and two thirds.

Ruby Walsh took his eleventh jockey's title with four wins, one second and three thirds, in spite of his unsuccessful first two days.

Robbie Power was second, with three wins. Six jockeys had two wins, with third place in the standings going to Noel Fehily, who also had three seconds and a third. Fourth place went to Bryan Cooper, who added one second and two thirds to his two wins.

Gigginstown House Stud topped the owners' list, with four wins.

The four days had seen the Cheltenham Festival at its best, and Ireland had not simply broken its previous Cheltenham record – it had smashed it. It was not all about the big stables, either.

The final score for 2017: Ireland 19 – England 9.

(The next day, for the record, Ireland dashed England's hoped-for record nineteenth consecutive Rugby Union test, winning by 13-9.)

BIBLIOGRAPHY

Arkle: The Legend of Himself

At Close Quarters: Dean Close School 1884–2009

Dawn Run: The story of a champion racehorse and her remarkable owner

Horses for Courses: An Irish Racing Year

In The Blood: Irish Racing Dynasties

Steeplechasing: A Celebration of 250 Years

Stride by Stride

Vincent O'Brien – The Official Biography

Carlow Nationalist

Daily Racing Form (USA)

New Ross Standard

The Daily Telegraph

The Guardian

The Independent

The Irish Field

The Sun

The Times

donnmcclean.com

gloucestershirelive.co.uk

goracing.ie (Horse Racing Ireland)

horseandhound.co.uk

independent.ie

dailymail.co.uk

ownerbreeder.co.uk

racingpost.com

racinguk.com

rte.ie/sport/racing

sportinglife.com

turtlebunbury.com

wpmullins.com

OTHER BOOKS BY ANNE HOLLAND
FROM THE O'BRIEN PRESS

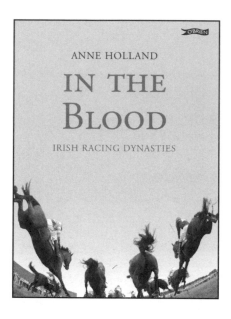

*'a truly startling picture of how interconnected
the racing tribe really is'*

Irish Examiner

'looks sure to be a winner'

Westmeath Examiner

A golden thread links diverse equine and human characters in Irish racing, past and present: generations of families in which racing is truly in the blood – or one-off fanatics who acquire it in their veins.

Not only trainers and jockeys, but also owners, breeders and the unsung heroes who care for their equine stars are portrayed here, as well as commentators and bookmakers, without whom the industry would be no more than a sideshow, instead of one of Ireland's greatest global products.

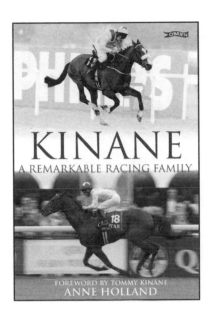

'a heart-warming story of a family who worked their way up from humble beginnings to worldwide fame'
Irish Racing Post

'a cracking read'
The Irish Field

Regarded by many as the perfect jockey, Mick Kinane rounded off his thirty-four-year career on a dazzling high with champion horse Sea The Stars, winning the 2,000 Guineas, Epsom Derby, the Eclipse Stakes, International Stakes, Irish Champion Stakes and Prix de l'Arc de Triomphe in 2009.

However, Mick is just one member of several generations of Kinanes who have consistently excelled in professional horse racing: through grit, talent and a legendary work ethic.

The backbone of Irish racing over the past fifty years, this is the story of a clan that includes National Hunt jockey Tommy, who won the Champion Hurdle on Monksfield and who once won a race despite a broken neck, and his sons Thomas, Jayo, Paul and of course Mick. The family has its roots in simpler and indeed harder times; this book tracks their rise to the pinnacle of their sport on the world stage.

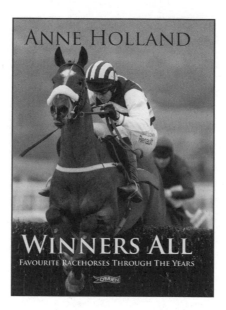

'the perfect gift for horse-racing enthusiasts'
The Irish Field

'well worth its place in any racing aficionado's library'
Sky Sports

The Byerley Turk * Eclipse * Bend Or * Manifesto * Cottage Rake * Jay Trump * Nijinksy * Golden Cygnet * Istabraq * Dorans Pride * Beef or Salmon * Moscow Flyer * Hardy Eustace * Makybe Diva * Zenyatta

Best-selling author and racing insider Anne Holland introduces her fifteen favourite racehorses. It is a dream line-up spanning three hundred years, from the great Byerley Turk, warhorse and ancestor of the thoroughbred line, to the steeplechasers and hurdlers of the twenty-first century. Anne's passion for her subject and extensive knowledge are undeniable, and the drama of a horse and its rider taking a fence or a jockey coaxing his mount to a thrilling finish will grip you.

Winners All recreates the times the sport of horse racing has captured imaginations and tells the stories not just of the horses, but also of their bloodlines, of the people behind their breeding and training and of the jockeys who rode them to their successes. This book is rich with entertaining anecdotes and tales of courage, grit and not a little glamour.

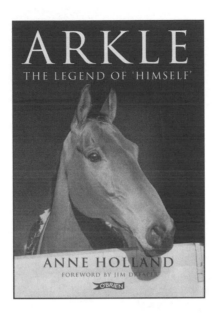

ARKLE
THE LEGEND OF 'HIMSELF'

ANNE HOLLAND
FOREWORD BY JIM DREAPER

'very entertaining … terrific book'
The Pat Kenny Show

'a wonderful reminder'
The Irish Echo

In 1964, Arkle's first-place finish in the Cheltenham Gold Cup was the first big win by Ireland's most celebrated racehorse: the horse by which all others are measured. Fifty years on from the start of his incredible career - which included wins in the Cheltenham Gold Cup (three times), Irish Grand National, Hennessy Gold Cup, King George VI Chase and Punchestown Gold Cup - Anne Holland looks at Arkle's life and legend through the eyes of those who knew him best.

She describes Arkle's career, his incredible wins, and the people involved with him, interviewing many of his connections, including Jim Dreaper, Paddy Woods, Tom Taaffe, sculptor Emma McDermott, the Baker family and others. Arkle was a star - the story goes that he received items of fan mail addressed to 'Himself, Ireland' - and this is a well-researched and intimate portrait of a legendary horse.

Shortlisted for Horse Racing Book of the Year 2014, British Sports Book Awards

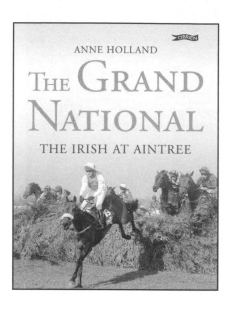

'sure to be a hit with any racing enthusiast.'
Belfast Newsletter

The Aintree Grand National is the world's most famous horserace – fast-paced, exhilarating and occasionally perilous. Everyone – serious racing fraternity and occasional flutterers alike – has heard of it. Millions are staked on the race, and millions watch. Down through the years it has produced many a fairytale result.

This lavishly-illustrated book examines the Irish presence at Aintree from the festival's earliest years; Irish horses, jockeys, trainers and breeders have always been prominent. No two horses have ever been trained alike for Aintree and no two stories have ever been the same. They are all here, written with the attention to detail and enthusiasm of a true racing fanatic. A wide-ranging and compulsively readable account of a beloved institution.